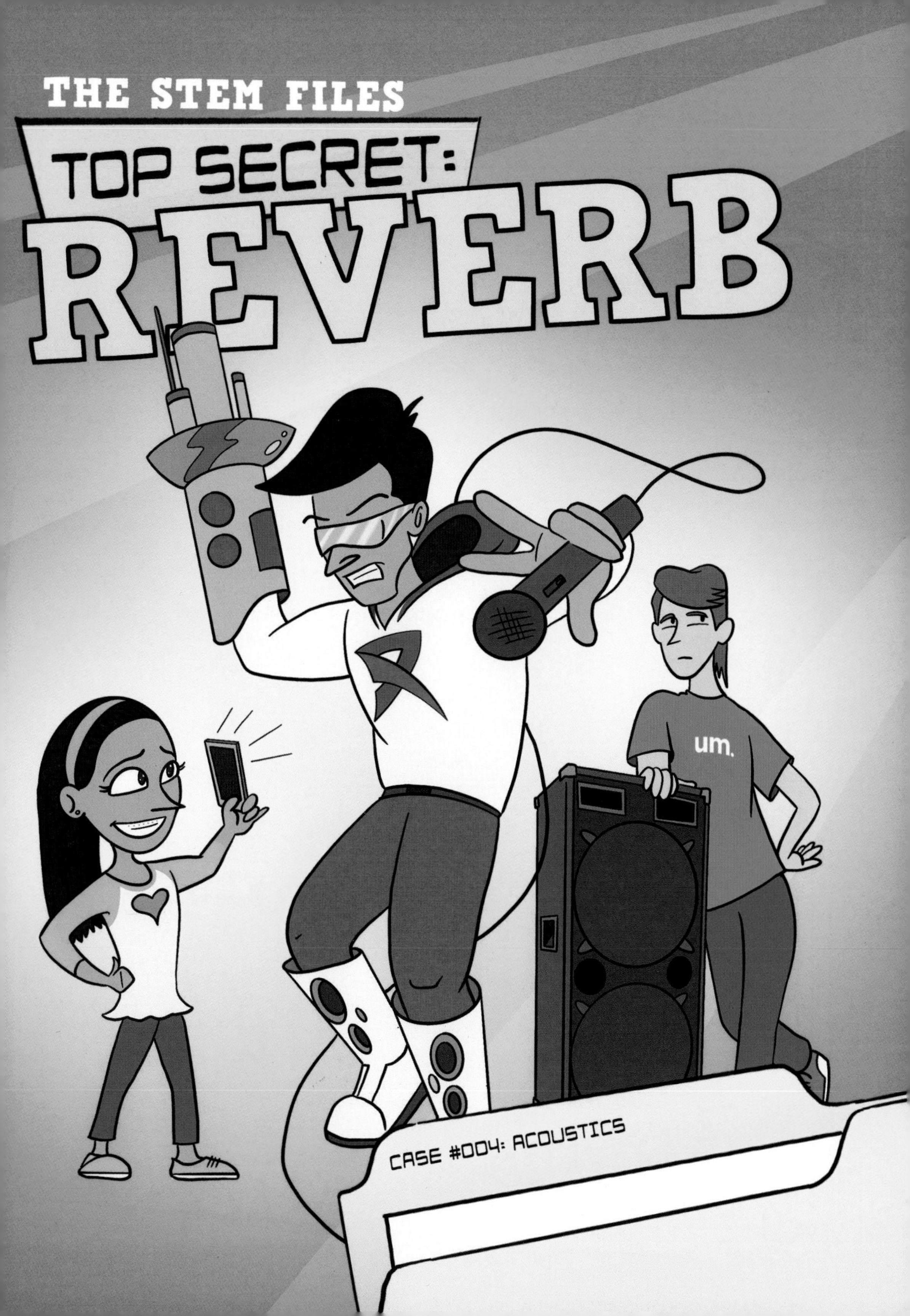
THE STEM FILES
TOP SECRET:
REVERB
um.
CASE #004: ACOUSTICS

TORCH GRAPHIC PRESS

Published in the United States of America by Cherry Lake Publishing Group
Ann Arbor, Michigan
www.cherrylakepublishing.com

Story & Illustrator: D.C. London
Character Design: John Boissy
Reading Adviser: Marla Conn, MS, Ed., Literacy specialist, Read-Ability, Inc.
Content Adviser: Bryan Choate, MS
Production Artists: Jen Wahi, Mary Wagner, Jessica Rogner

Torch Graphic Press is an imprint of Cherry Lake Publishing Group.

Library of Congress Cataloging-in-Publication Data

Names: London, D. C., author.
Title: Top secret: Reverb / written by D.C. London.
Other titles: Reverb
Description: Ann Arbor, Michigan : Cherry Lake Publishing, [2020] | Series:
    The STEM files | Includes bibliographical references and index. |
Identifiers: LCCN 2020007009 (print) | LCCN 2020007010 (ebook) | ISBN
    9781534169333 (hardcover) | ISBN 9781534171015 (paperback) | ISBN
    9781534172852 (pdf) | ISBN 9781534174696 (ebook)
Subjects: LCSH: Graphic novels. | CYAC: Graphic novels. | Sound
    waves--Fiction. | Revenge--Fiction. | Villains--Fiction.
Classification: LCC PZ7.7.L663 Tor 2020 (print) | LCC PZ7.7.L663 (ebook)
    | DDC 741.5/973--dc23
LC record available at https://lccn.loc.gov/2020007009
LC ebook record available at https://lccn.loc.gov/2020007010

Cherry Lake Publishing Group would like to acknowledge the work of the
Partnership for 21st Century Learning, a Network of Battelle for Kids.
Please visit http://www.battelleforkids.org/networks/p21 for more information.

Printed in the United States of America
Corporate Graphics

About the Artist: D.C. London
Mr. London is an author, illustrator, designer, part-time Samurai, Army veteran,
former rocket scientist, and tank blower-upper. He blatantly violates child labor
laws by forcing his three young sons to read his silly books and tests bad jokes on
them without proper protective gear.

Table of Contents

A Note on STEM and Sound
STEM stands for science, technology, engineering, and mathematics.
In this book, you will learn about what sound is, how it works, and the
different ways sound is used.

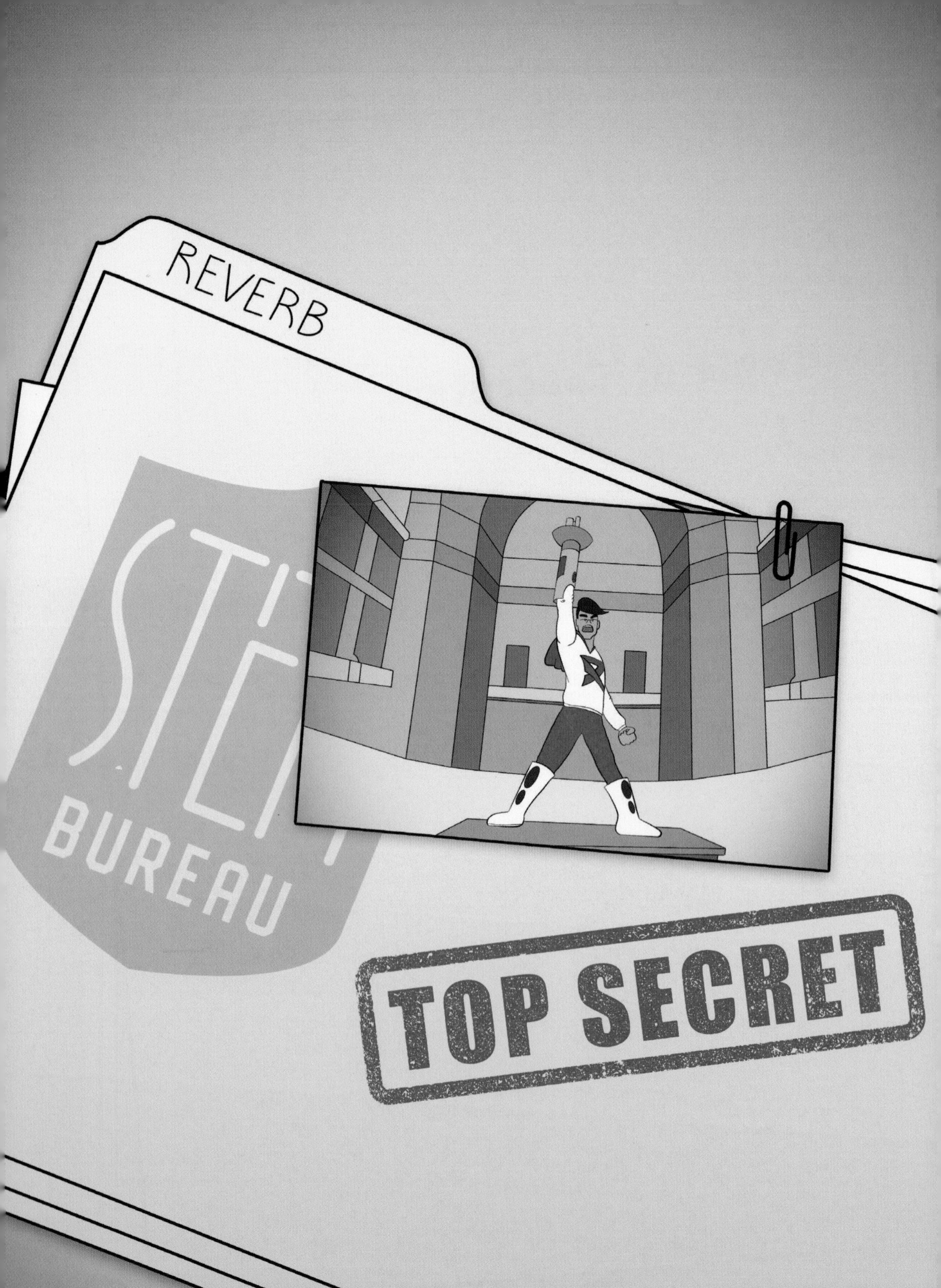
REVERB
S.T.E.M. BUREAU
TOP SECRET

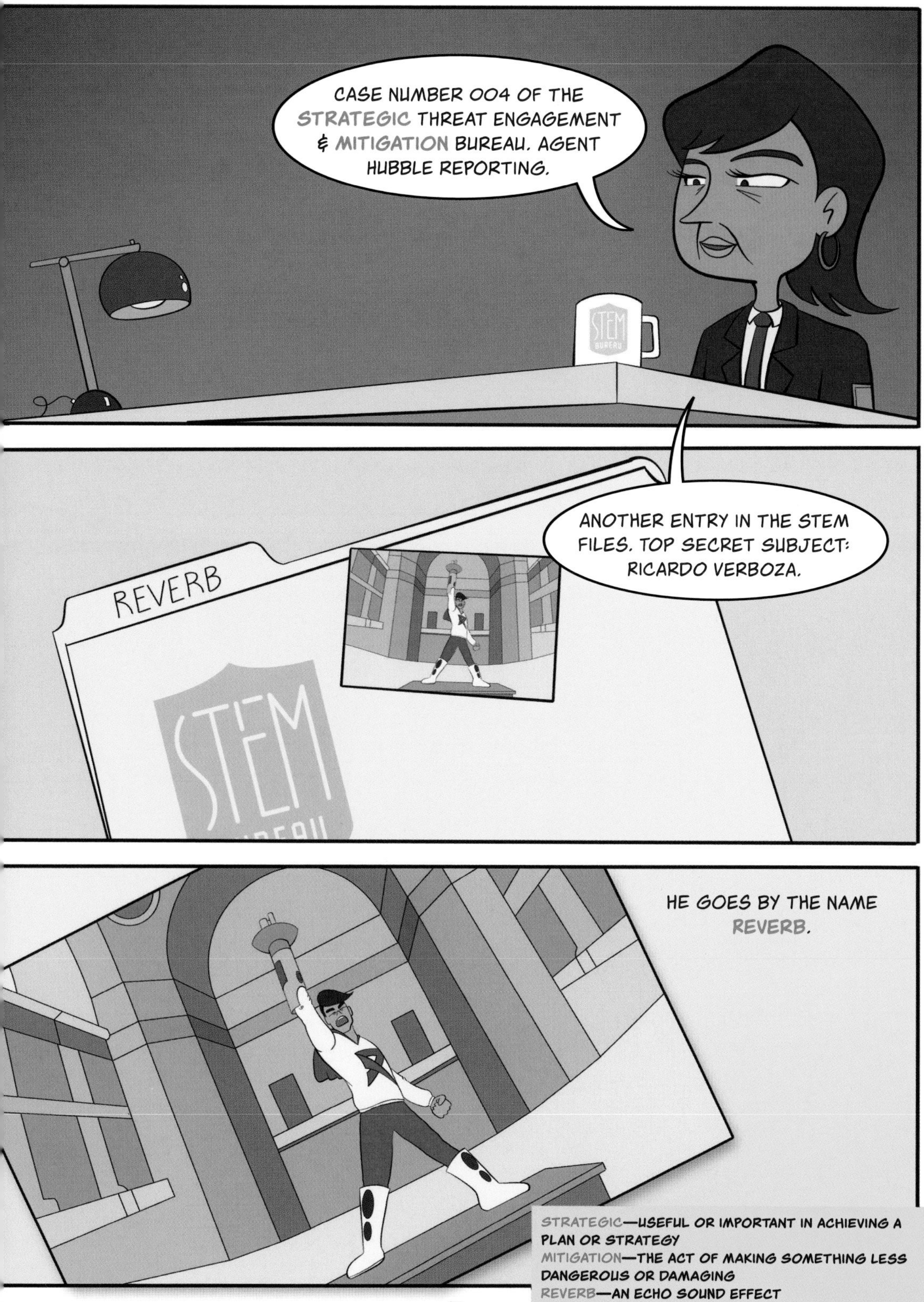
CASE NUMBER 004 OF THE STRATEGIC THREAT ENGAGEMENT & MITIGATION BUREAU. AGENT HUBBLE REPORTING.
ANOTHER ENTRY IN THE STEM FILES. TOP SECRET SUBJECT: RICARDO VERBOZA.
REVERB
HE GOES BY THE NAME REVERB.

STRATEGIC—USEFUL OR IMPORTANT IN ACHIEVING A PLAN OR STRATEGY
MITIGATION—THE ACT OF MAKING SOMETHING LESS DANGEROUS OR DAMAGING
REVERB—AN ECHO SOUND EFFECT

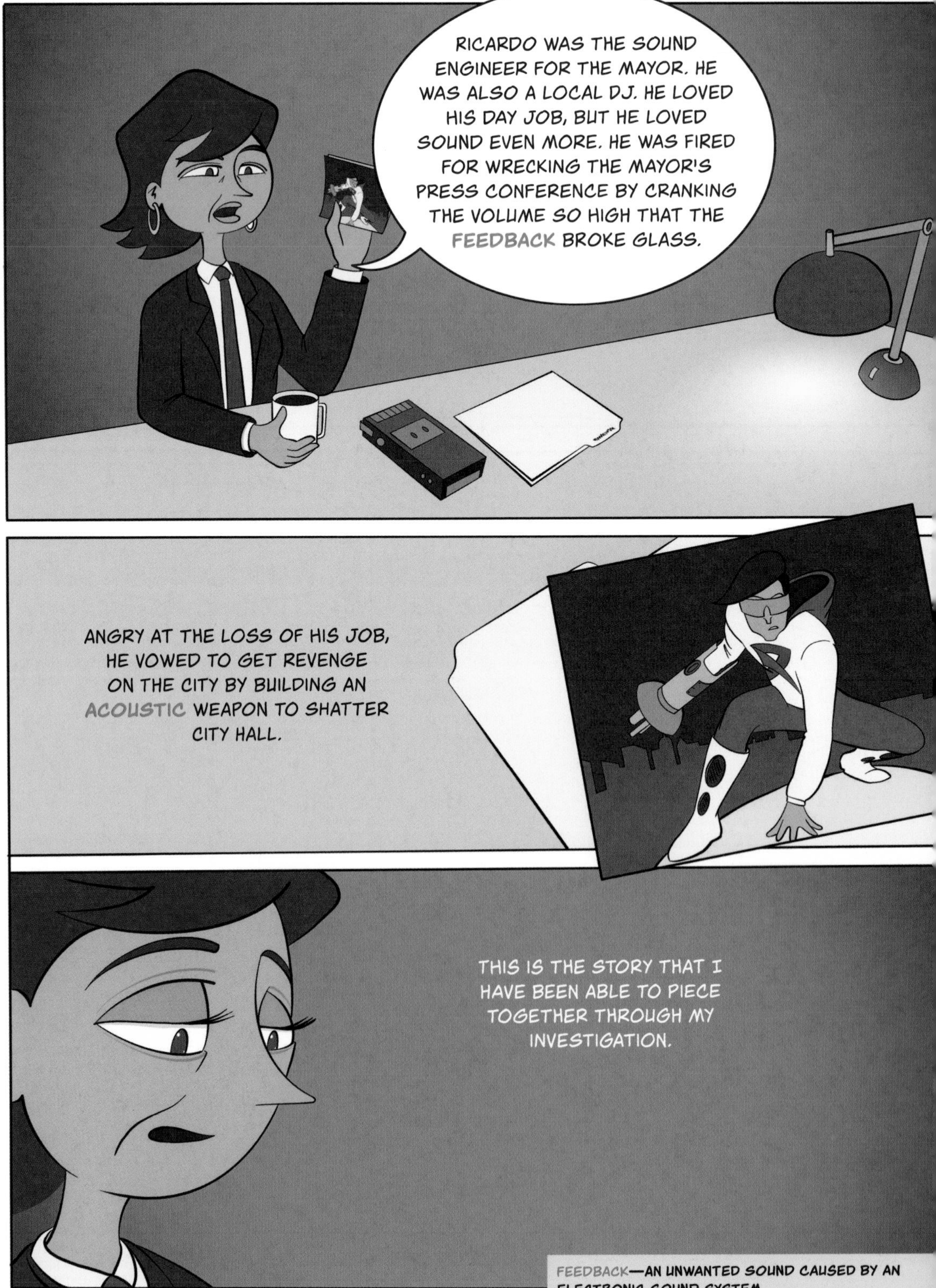
RICARDO WAS THE SOUND ENGINEER FOR THE MAYOR. HE WAS ALSO A LOCAL DJ. HE LOVED HIS DAY JOB, BUT HE LOVED SOUND EVEN MORE. HE WAS FIRED FOR WRECKING THE MAYOR'S PRESS CONFERENCE BY CRANKING THE VOLUME SO HIGH THAT THE FEEDBACK BROKE GLASS.
ANGRY AT THE LOSS OF HIS JOB, HE VOWED TO GET REVENGE ON THE CITY BY BUILDING AN ACOUSTIC WEAPON TO SHATTER CITY HALL.
THIS IS THE STORY THAT I HAVE BEEN ABLE TO PIECE TOGETHER THROUGH MY INVESTIGATION.

FEEDBACK—AN UNWANTED SOUND CAUSED BY AN ELECTRONIC SOUND SYSTEM
ACOUSTIC—RELATING TO SOUND

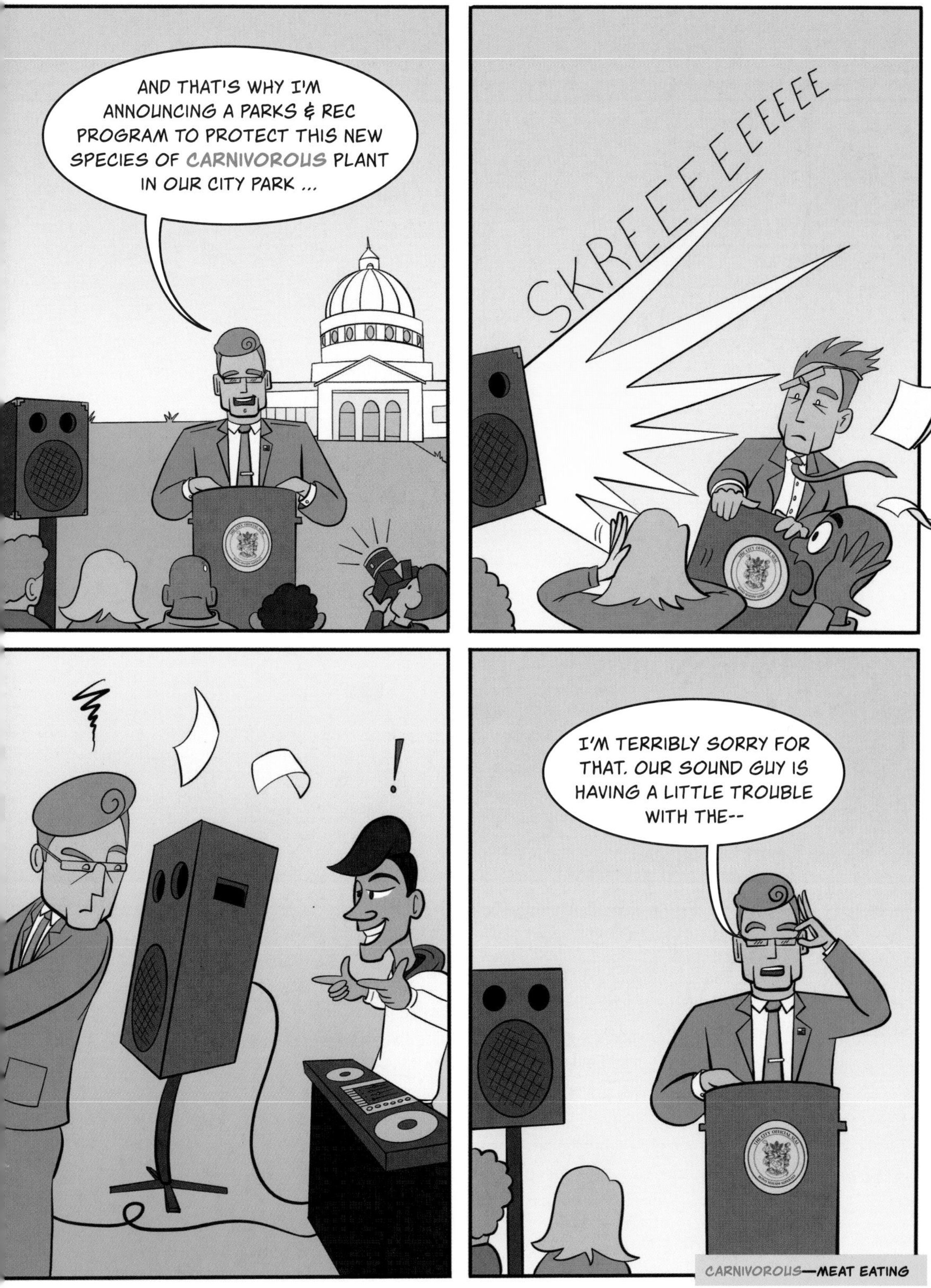
AND THAT'S WHY I'M ANNOUNCING A PARKS & REC PROGRAM TO PROTECT THIS NEW SPECIES OF CARNIVOROUS PLANT IN OUR CITY PARK ...
SKREEEEEEEEEE
!
I'M TERRIBLY SORRY FOR THAT. OUR SOUND GUY IS HAVING A LITTLE TROUBLE WITH THE--
CARNIVOROUS—MEAT EATING

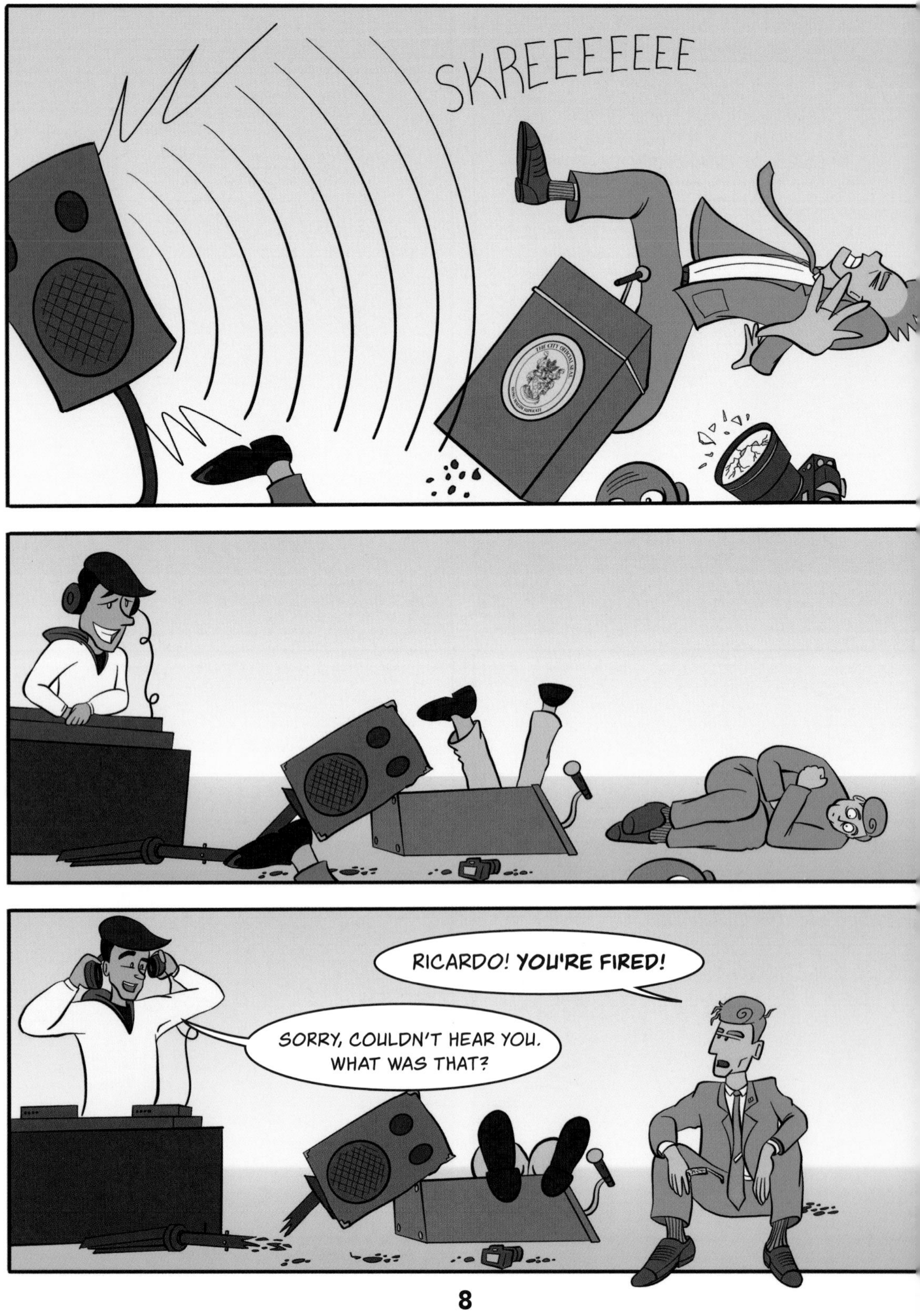
SKREEEEEEE
RICARDO! **YOU'RE FIRED!**
SORRY, COULDN'T HEAR YOU. WHAT WAS THAT?

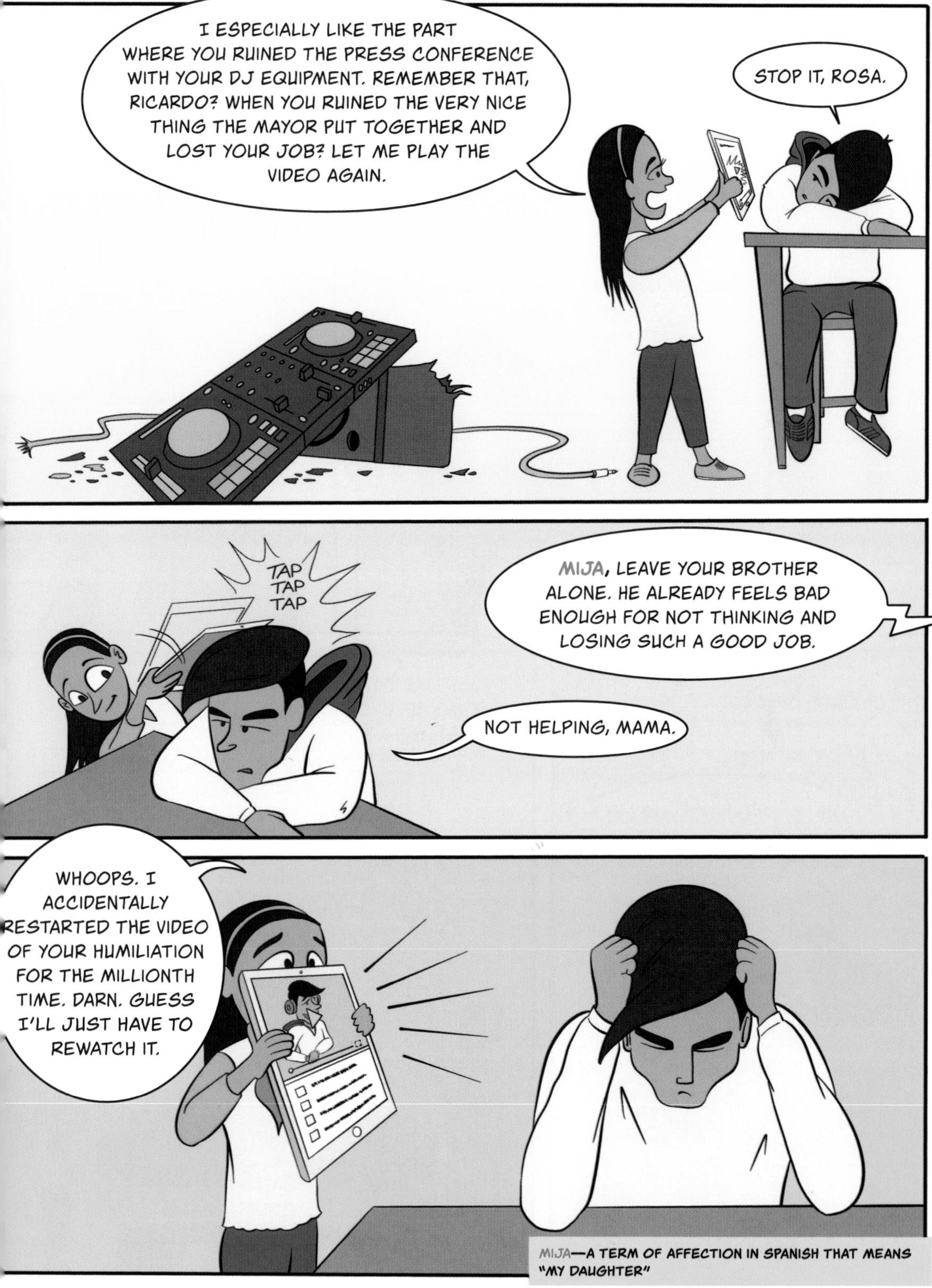
I ESPECIALLY LIKE THE PART WHERE YOU RUINED THE PRESS CONFERENCE WITH YOUR DJ EQUIPMENT. REMEMBER THAT, RICARDO? WHEN YOU RUINED THE VERY NICE THING THE MAYOR PUT TOGETHER AND LOST YOUR JOB? LET ME PLAY THE VIDEO AGAIN.
STOP IT, ROSA.
TAP TAP TAP
MIJA, LEAVE YOUR BROTHER ALONE. HE ALREADY FEELS BAD ENOUGH FOR NOT THINKING AND LOSING SUCH A GOOD JOB.
NOT HELPING, MAMA.
WHOOPS. I ACCIDENTALLY RESTARTED THE VIDEO OF YOUR HUMILIATION FOR THE MILLIONTH TIME. DARN. GUESS I'LL JUST HAVE TO REWATCH IT.

MIJA—A TERM OF AFFECTION IN SPANISH THAT MEANS "MY DAUGHTER"

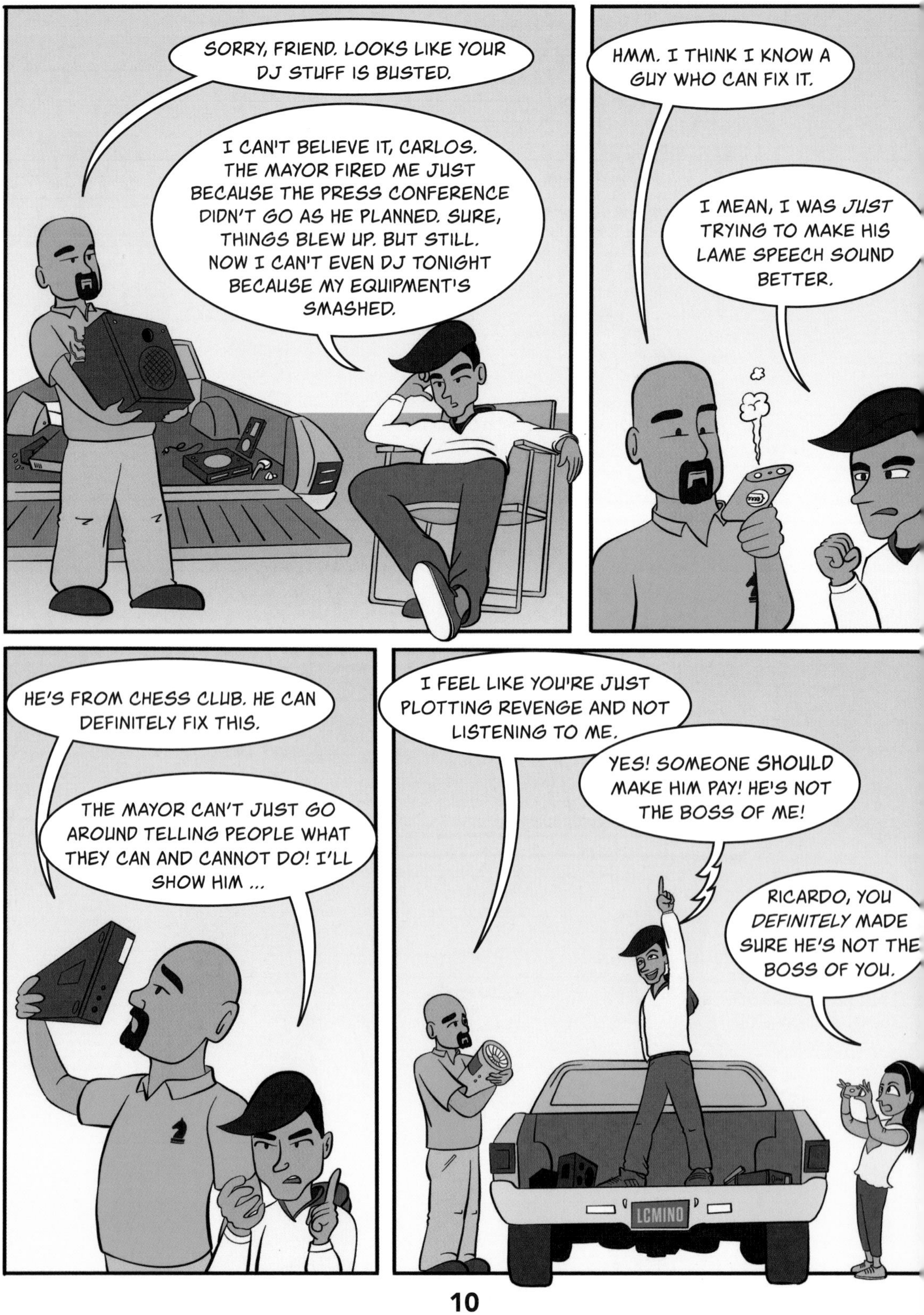
SORRY, FRIEND. LOOKS LIKE YOUR DJ STUFF IS BUSTED.
I CAN'T BELIEVE IT, CARLOS. THE MAYOR FIRED ME JUST BECAUSE THE PRESS CONFERENCE DIDN'T GO AS HE PLANNED. SURE, THINGS BLEW UP. BUT STILL. NOW I CAN'T EVEN DJ TONIGHT BECAUSE MY EQUIPMENT'S SMASHED.
HMM. I THINK I KNOW A GUY WHO CAN FIX IT.
I MEAN, I WAS *JUST* TRYING TO MAKE HIS LAME SPEECH SOUND BETTER.
HE'S FROM CHESS CLUB. HE CAN DEFINITELY FIX THIS.
THE MAYOR CAN'T JUST GO AROUND TELLING PEOPLE WHAT THEY CAN AND CANNOT DO! I'LL SHOW HIM ...
I FEEL LIKE YOU'RE JUST PLOTTING REVENGE AND NOT LISTENING TO ME.
YES! SOMEONE SHOULD MAKE HIM PAY! HE'S NOT THE BOSS OF ME!
RICARDO, YOU *DEFINITELY* MADE SURE HE'S NOT THE BOSS OF YOU.
LCMINO

How Sound Works

Sound is an output of a vibrating object. An output is something produced. Vibrations are a series of continuous tiny movements. The object's vibrating motion causes the molecules in the surrounding environment, such as air and water, to also vibrate. Because of this cause and effect, energy—specifically sound energy—travels from one area to another. For instance, when a person plucks the strings of a guitar, those vibrating strings cause the molecules around it to also vibrate. These vibrating molecules then cause other neighboring molecules to vibrate. This series of vibrating molecules is what moves sound from one area to another.

However, as sound energy travels from one area to another, its energy slowly declines. As the energy declines, so does the number of vibrating molecules. This decline eventually causes sound to fade away. This explains why the farther away you are from an object, the fainter the noise is. Because greater distances require substantially more vibrating molecules to transmit sound, it is no wonder why sound quickly fades the farther you move away from the source!

um.

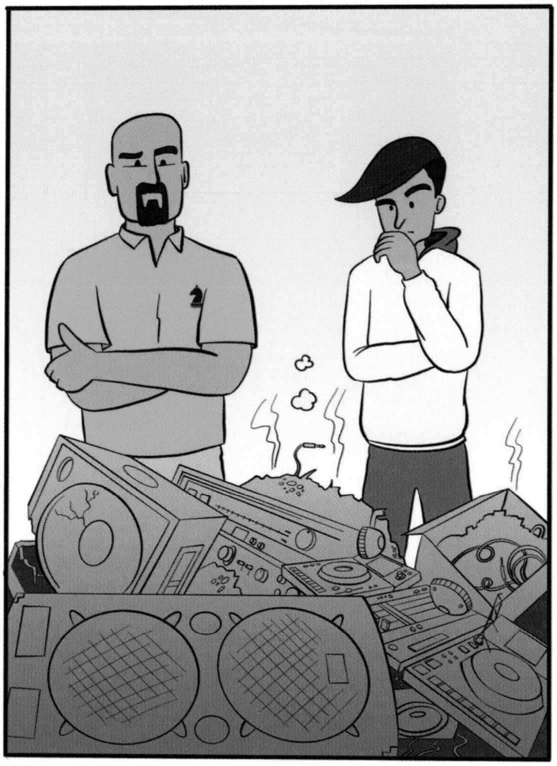

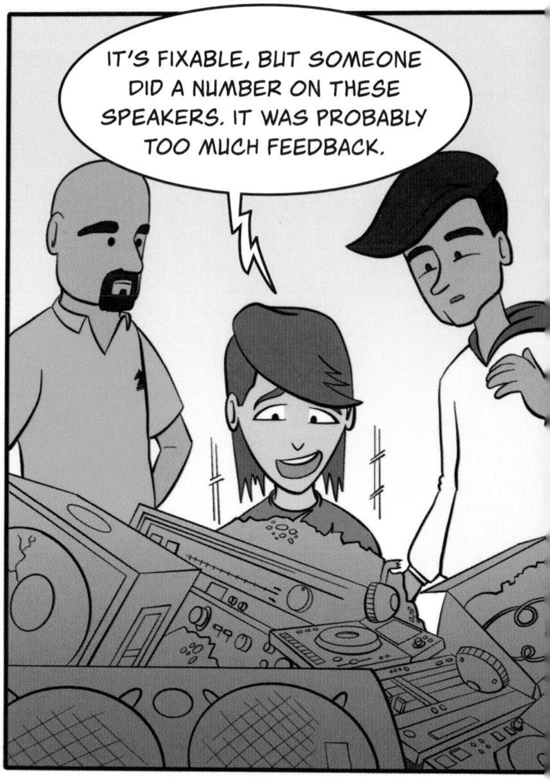
IT'S FIXABLE, BUT SOMEONE DID A NUMBER ON THESE SPEAKERS. IT WAS PROBABLY TOO MUCH FEEDBACK.

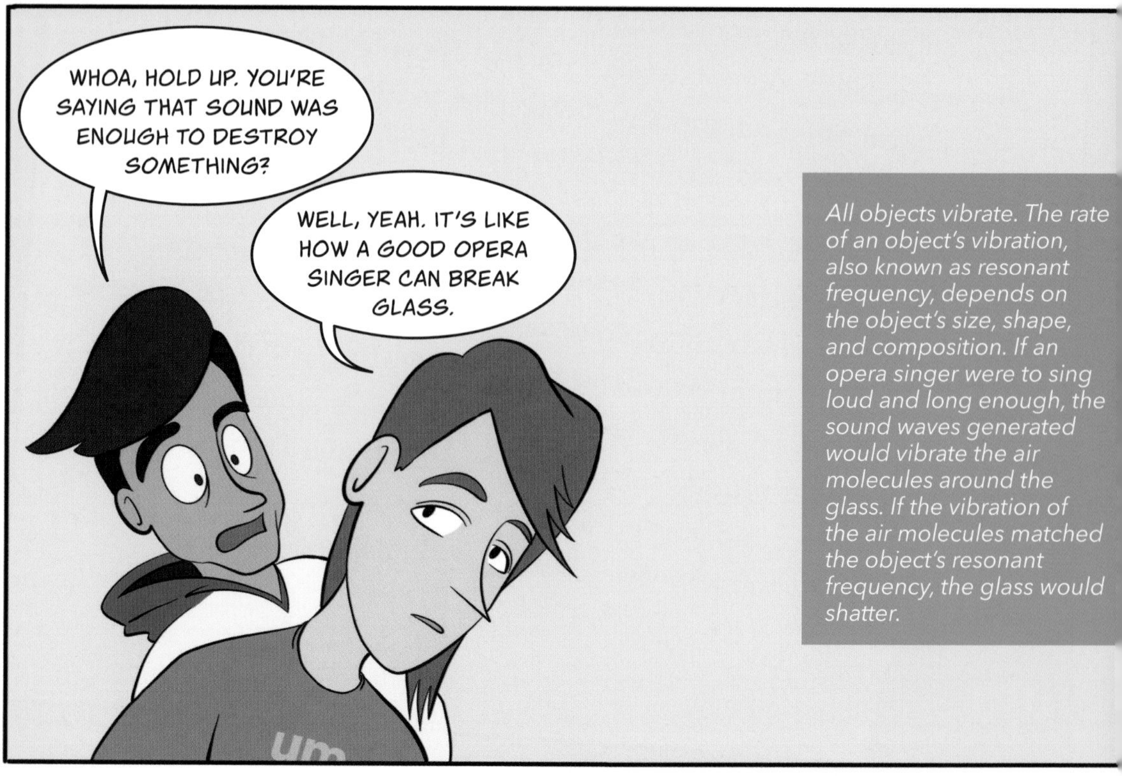
WHOA, HOLD UP. YOU'RE SAYING THAT SOUND WAS ENOUGH TO DESTROY SOMETHING?
WELL, YEAH. IT'S LIKE HOW A GOOD OPERA SINGER CAN BREAK GLASS.
All objects vibrate. The rate of an object's vibration, also known as resonant frequency, depends on the object's size, shape, and composition. If an opera singer were to sing loud and long enough, the sound waves generated would vibrate the air molecules around the glass. If the vibration of the air molecules matched the object's resonant frequency, the glass would shatter.

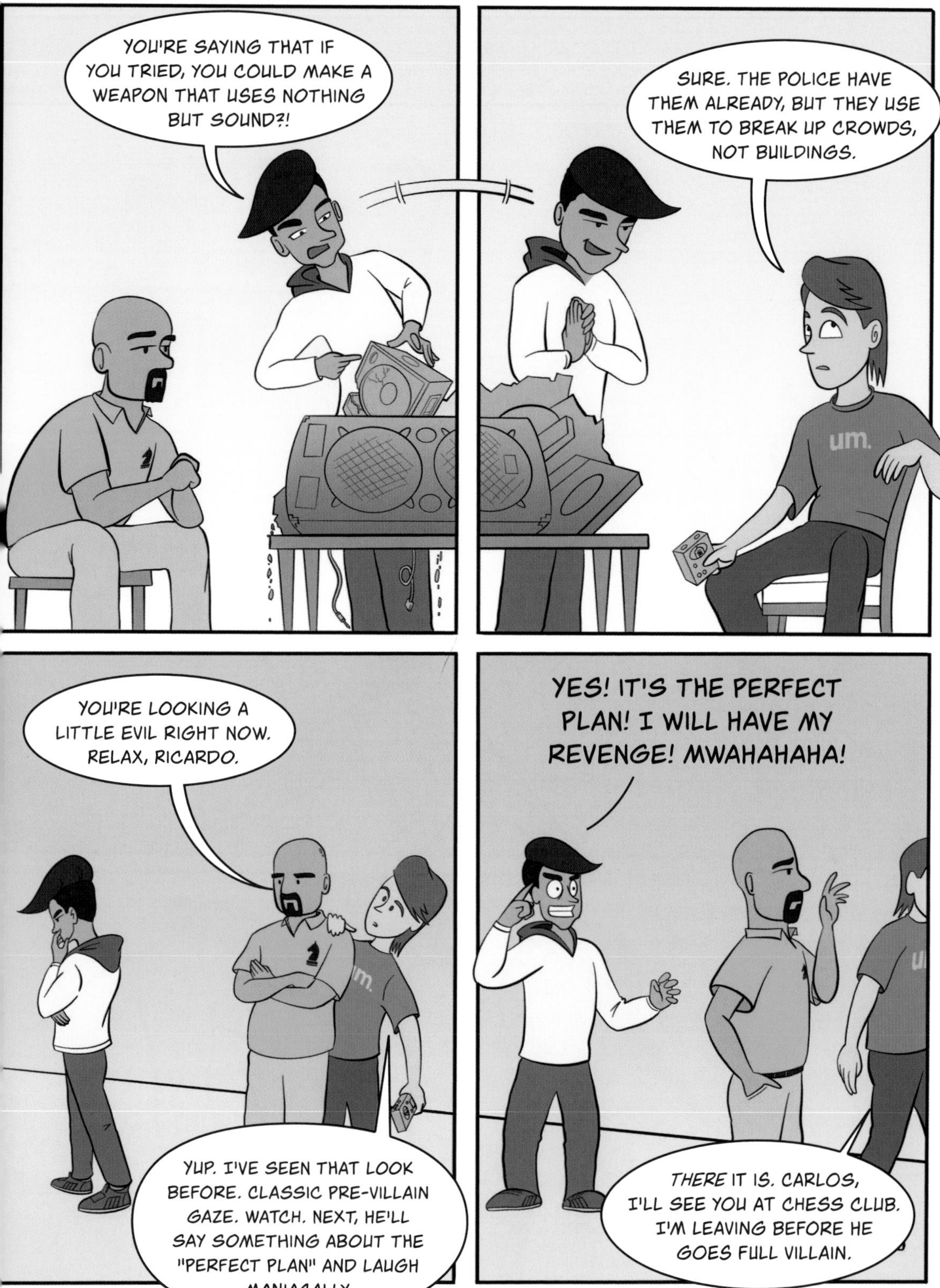
YOU'RE SAYING THAT IF YOU TRIED, YOU COULD MAKE A WEAPON THAT USES NOTHING BUT SOUND?!
SURE. THE POLICE HAVE THEM ALREADY, BUT THEY USE THEM TO BREAK UP CROWDS, NOT BUILDINGS.
um.
YOU'RE LOOKING A LITTLE EVIL RIGHT NOW. RELAX, RICARDO.
YUP. I'VE SEEN THAT LOOK BEFORE. CLASSIC PRE-VILLAIN GAZE. WATCH. NEXT, HE'LL SAY SOMETHING ABOUT THE "PERFECT PLAN" AND LAUGH MANIACALLY.
um.
YES! IT'S THE PERFECT PLAN! I WILL HAVE MY REVENGE! MWAHAHAHA!
THERE IT IS. CARLOS, I'LL SEE YOU AT CHESS CLUB. I'M LEAVING BEFORE HE GOES FULL VILLAIN.

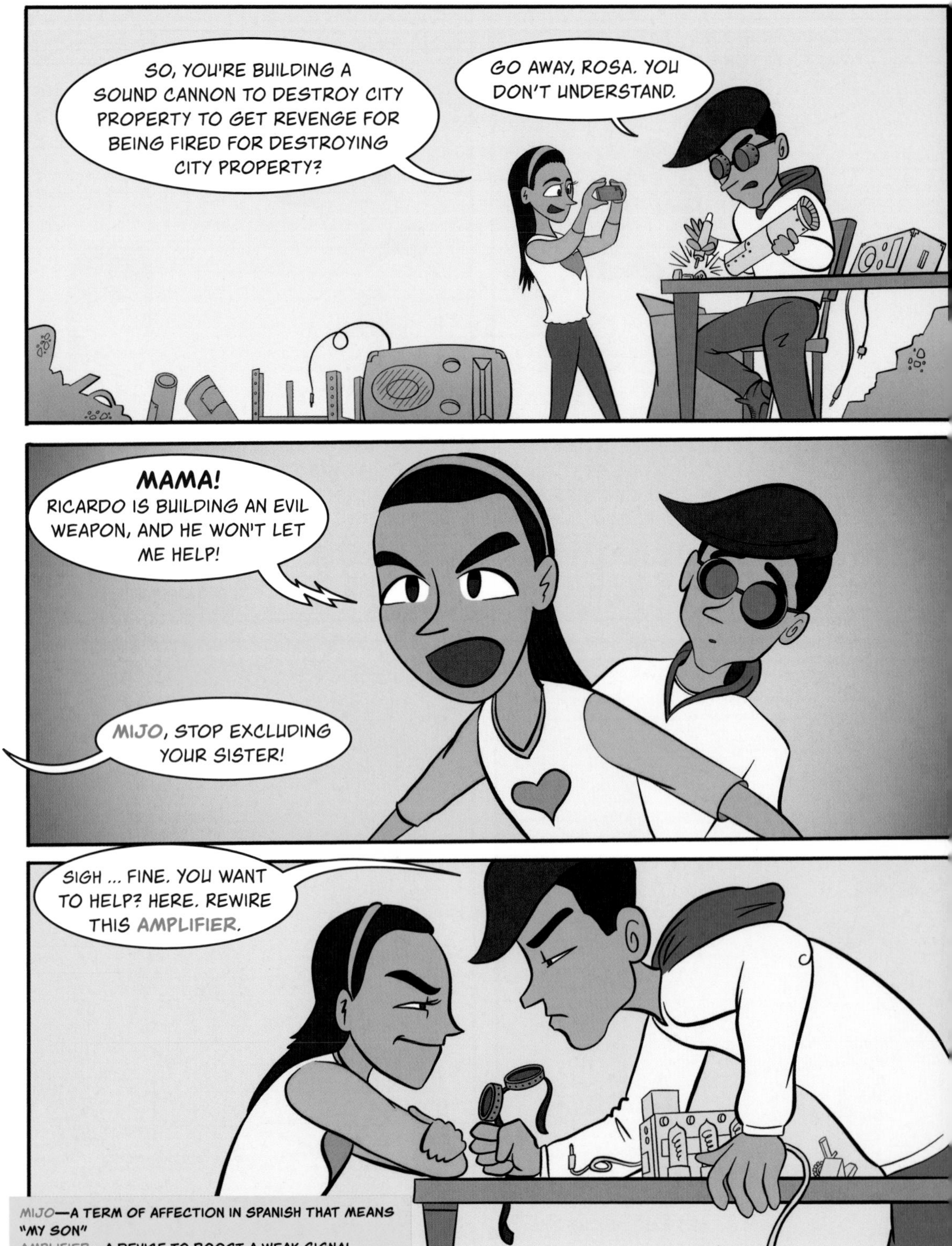
SO, YOU'RE BUILDING A SOUND CANNON TO DESTROY CITY PROPERTY TO GET REVENGE FOR BEING FIRED FOR DESTROYING CITY PROPERTY?
GO AWAY, ROSA. YOU DON'T UNDERSTAND.
MAMA! RICARDO IS BUILDING AN EVIL WEAPON, AND HE WON'T LET ME HELP!
MIJO, STOP EXCLUDING YOUR SISTER!
SIGH ... FINE. YOU WANT TO HELP? HERE. REWIRE THIS AMPLIFIER.

MIJO—A TERM OF AFFECTION IN SPANISH THAT MEANS "MY SON"
AMPLIFIER—A DEVICE TO BOOST A WEAK SIGNAL WITHOUT CHANGING IT

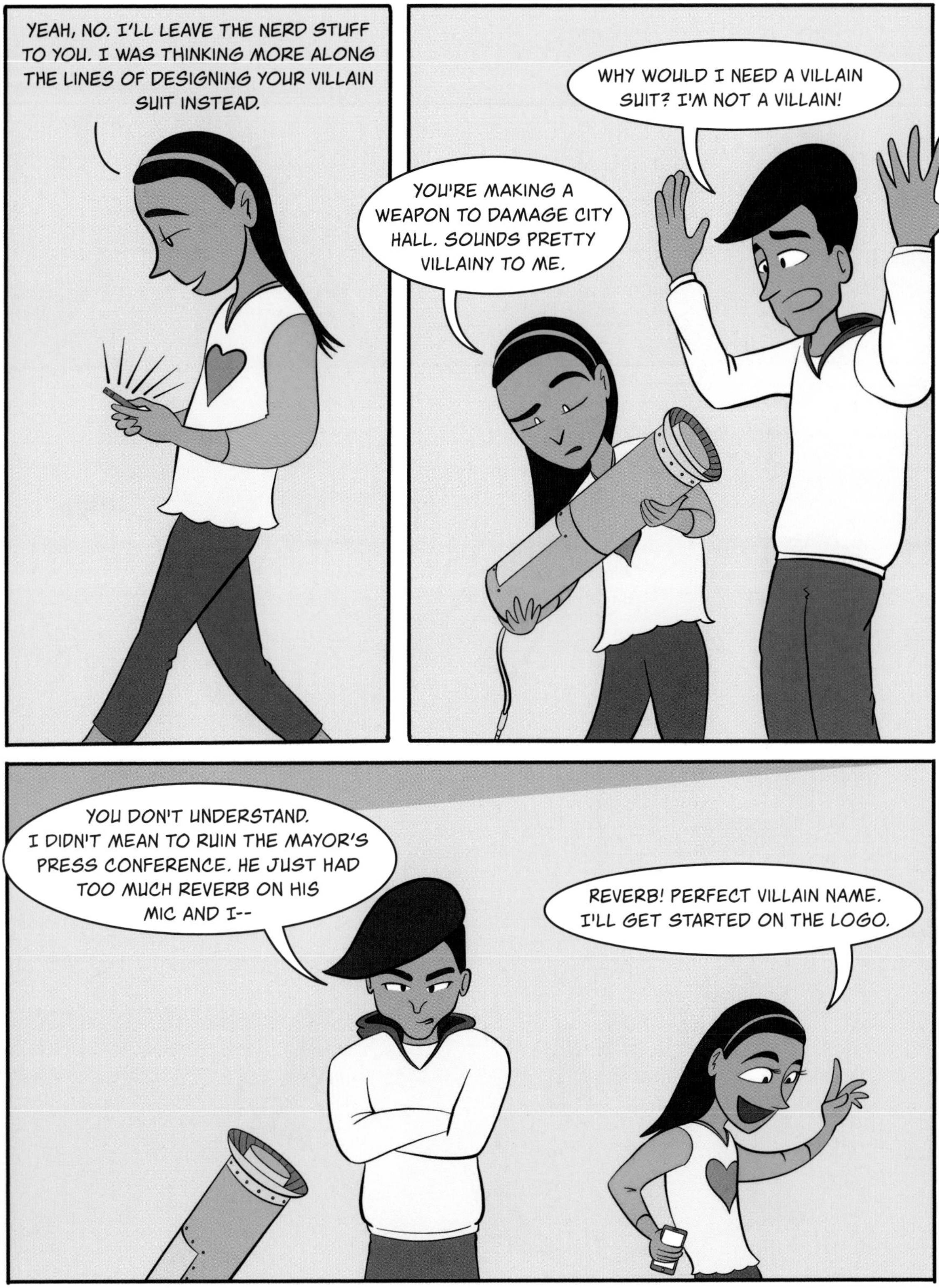
YEAH, NO. I'LL LEAVE THE NERD STUFF TO YOU. I WAS THINKING MORE ALONG THE LINES OF DESIGNING YOUR VILLAIN SUIT INSTEAD.
WHY WOULD I NEED A VILLAIN SUIT? I'M NOT A VILLAIN!
YOU'RE MAKING A WEAPON TO DAMAGE CITY HALL. SOUNDS PRETTY VILLAINY TO ME.
YOU DON'T UNDERSTAND. I DIDN'T MEAN TO RUIN THE MAYOR'S PRESS CONFERENCE. HE JUST HAD TOO MUCH REVERB ON HIS MIC AND I--
REVERB! PERFECT VILLAIN NAME. I'LL GET STARTED ON THE LOGO.

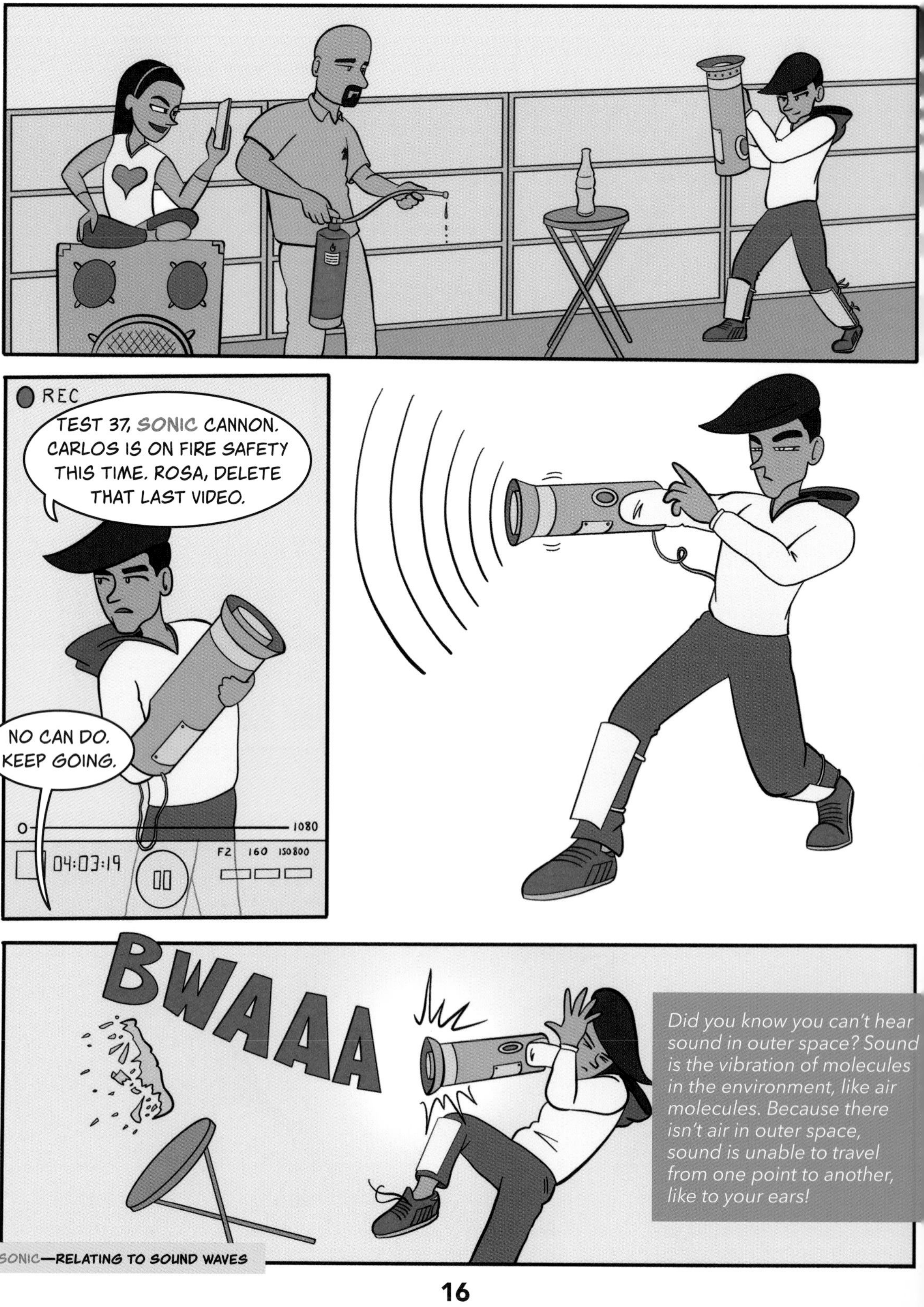
REC
TEST 37, SONIC CANNON. CARLOS IS ON FIRE SAFETY THIS TIME. ROSA, DELETE THAT LAST VIDEO.
NO CAN DO. KEEP GOING.
0
1080
04:03:19
F2 160 ISO800
BWAAA
Did you know you can't hear sound in outer space? Sound is the vibration of molecules in the environment, like air molecules. Because there isn't air in outer space, sound is unable to travel from one point to another, like to your ears!

SONIC—RELATING TO SOUND WAVES

Ways Sound Is Used

Sound is primarily used for audible (hearing) communication. But did you know it can be used for so much more? Sound waves can be used to move objects with acoustic levitation. Photos can be taken inside the body for medical purposes using ultrasound. Sound waves can even locate objects underwater through the use of sonar.

Acoustic levitation works by focusing sound waves on a single object. This focus applies a physical pressure on the object's surface. With enough focused pressure, the object levitates, or floats! On the other hand, ultrasound works by sending high frequency sound pulses into the body. When a sound pulse hits a boundary—like fluid, soft tissue, or bone—it bounces back. This bounce back is received, interpreted, and re-created into an image via the ultrasound machine. Similarly, sonar works by transmitting sound waves into the environment using an echo machine. As the sound waves bounce off nearby objects and are reflected back, their location can be determined relative to the echo machine.

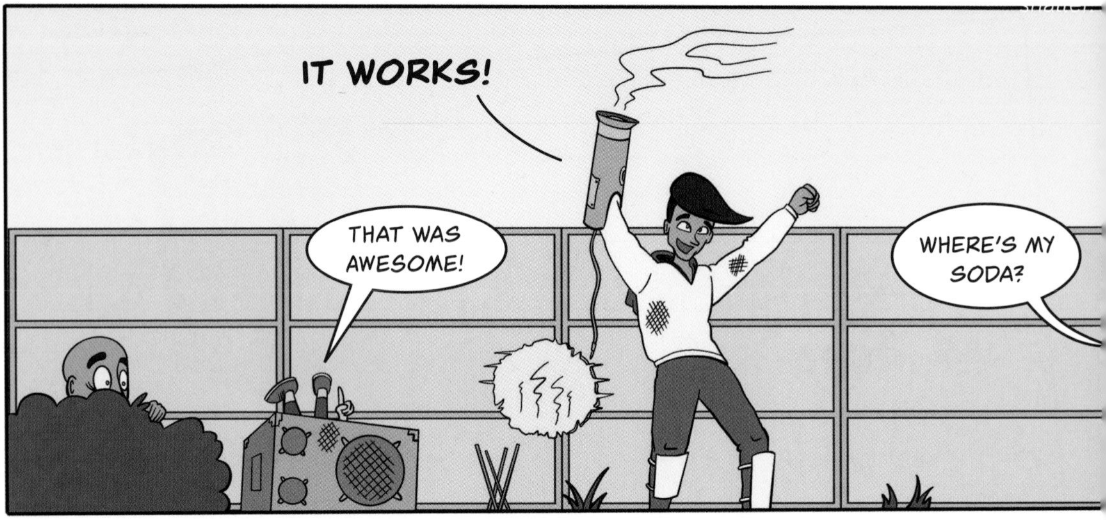
IT WORKS!
THAT WAS AWESOME!
WHERE'S MY SODA?

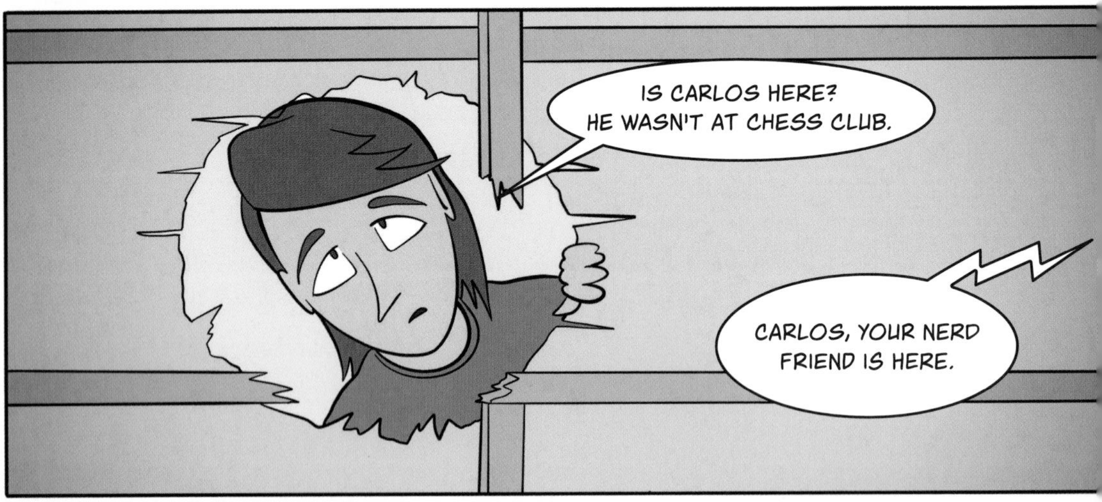
IS CARLOS HERE? HE WASN'T AT CHESS CLUB.
CARLOS, YOUR NERD FRIEND IS HERE.

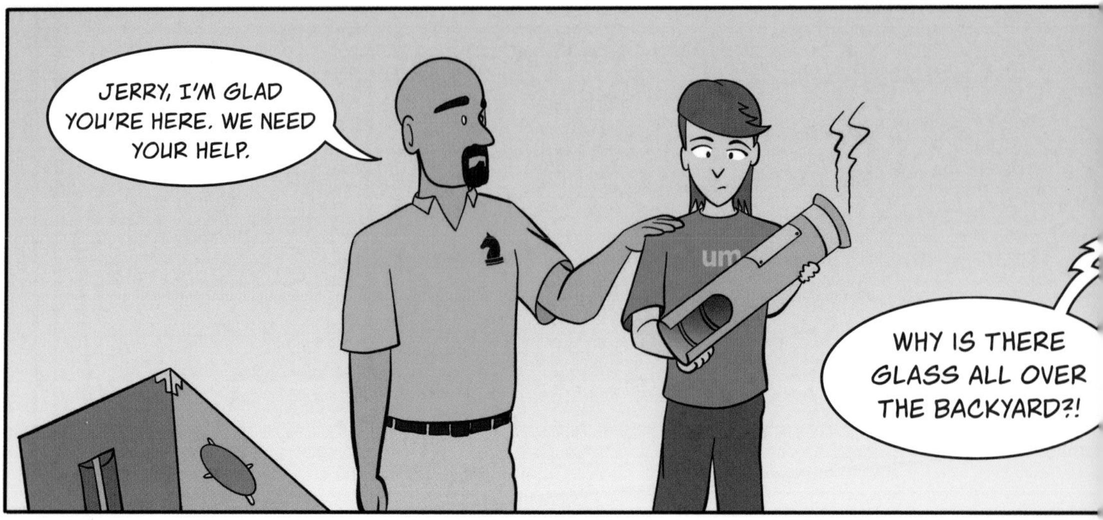
JERRY, I'M GLAD YOU'RE HERE. WE NEED YOUR HELP.
WHY IS THERE GLASS ALL OVER THE BACKYARD?!

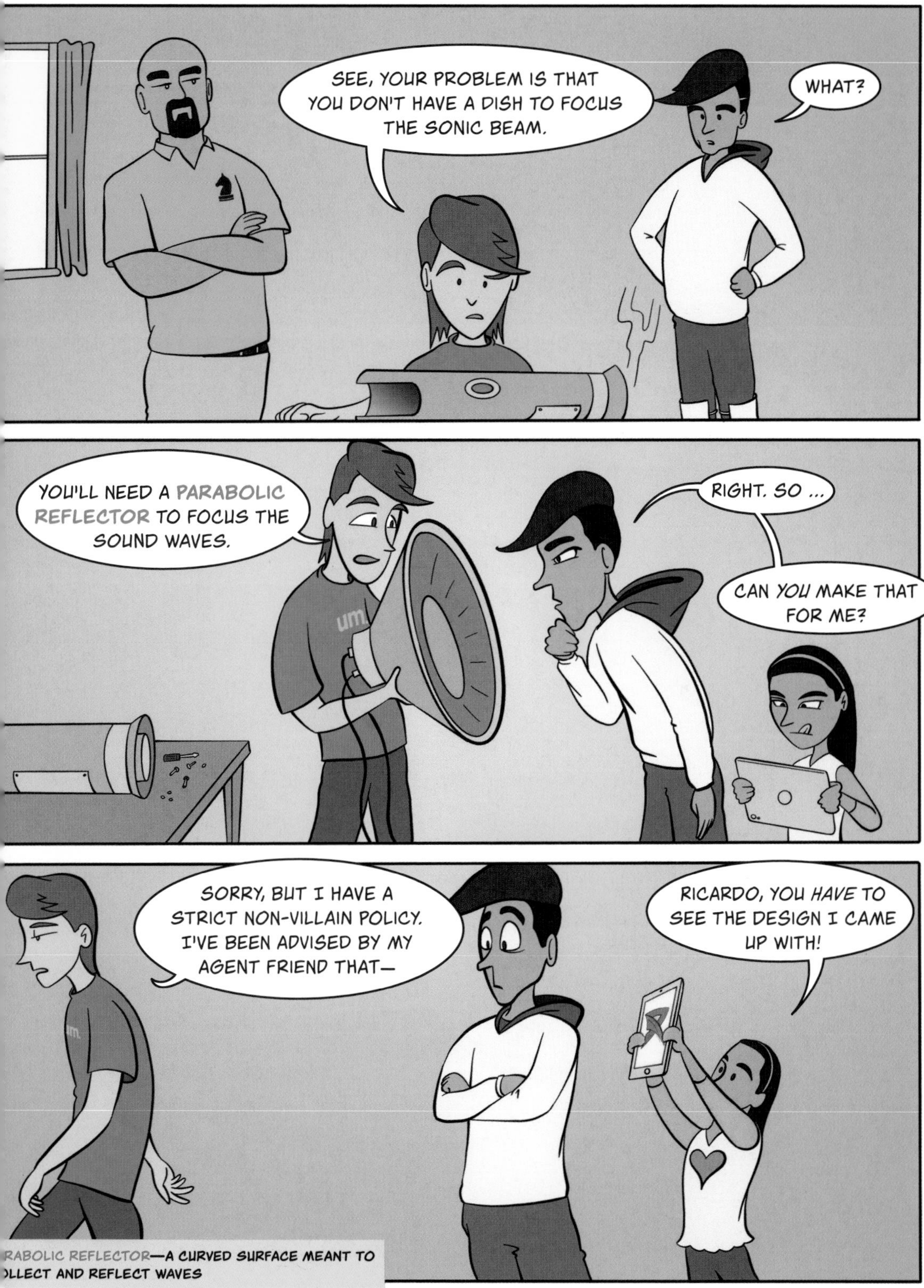
SEE, YOUR PROBLEM IS THAT YOU DON'T HAVE A DISH TO FOCUS THE SONIC BEAM.
WHAT?
YOU'LL NEED A PARABOLIC REFLECTOR TO FOCUS THE SOUND WAVES.
RIGHT. SO ...
CAN YOU MAKE THAT FOR ME?
SORRY, BUT I HAVE A STRICT NON-VILLAIN POLICY. I'VE BEEN ADVISED BY MY AGENT FRIEND THAT—
RICARDO, YOU HAVE TO SEE THE DESIGN I CAME UP WITH!
um.

RABOLIC REFLECTOR—A CURVED SURFACE MEANT TO
LLECT AND REFLECT WAVES

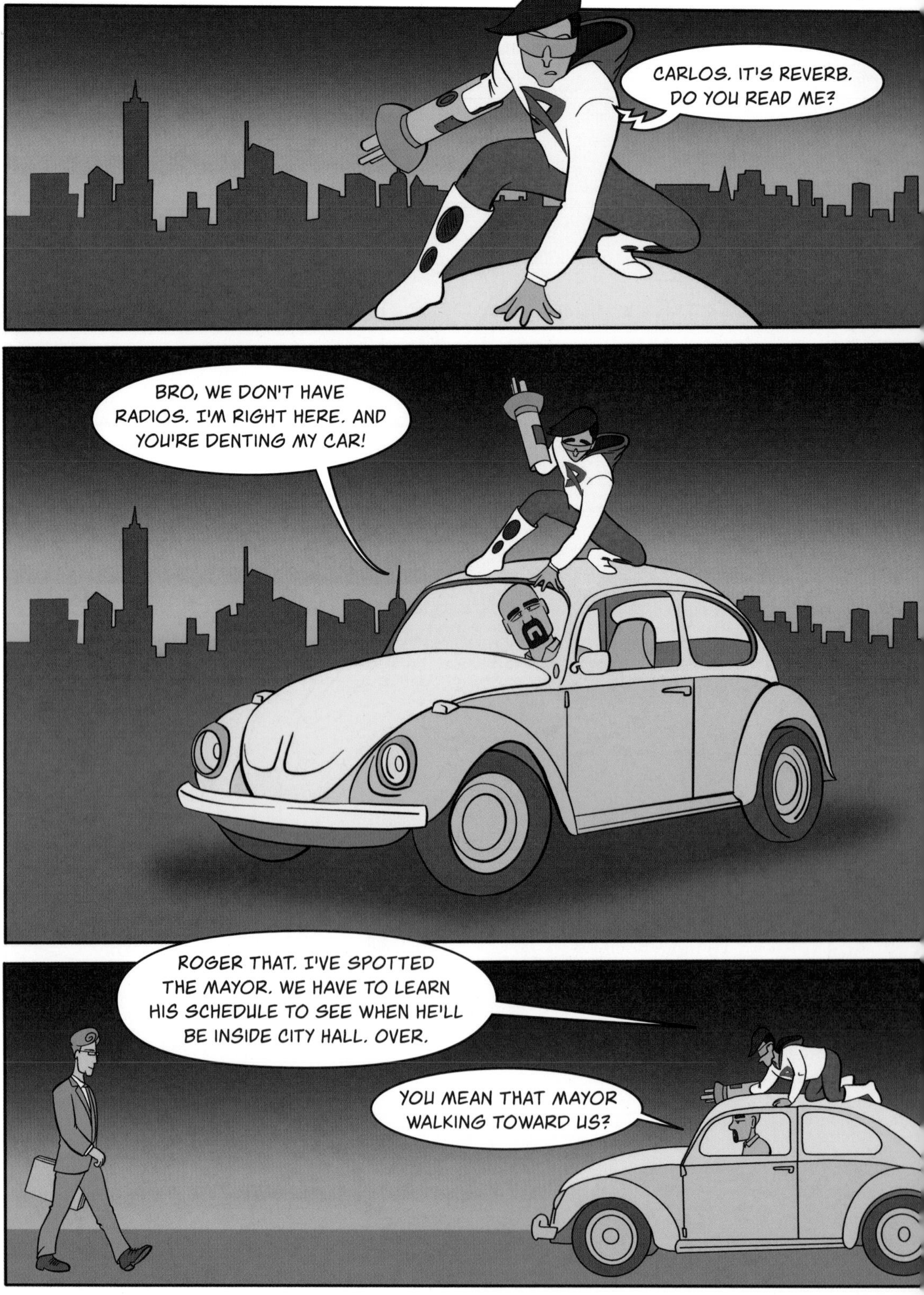
CARLOS. IT'S REVERB. DO YOU READ ME?
BRO, WE DON'T HAVE RADIOS. I'M RIGHT HERE. AND YOU'RE DENTING MY CAR!
ROGER THAT. I'VE SPOTTED THE MAYOR. WE HAVE TO LEARN HIS SCHEDULE TO SEE WHEN HE'LL BE INSIDE CITY HALL. OVER.
YOU MEAN THAT MAYOR WALKING TOWARD US?

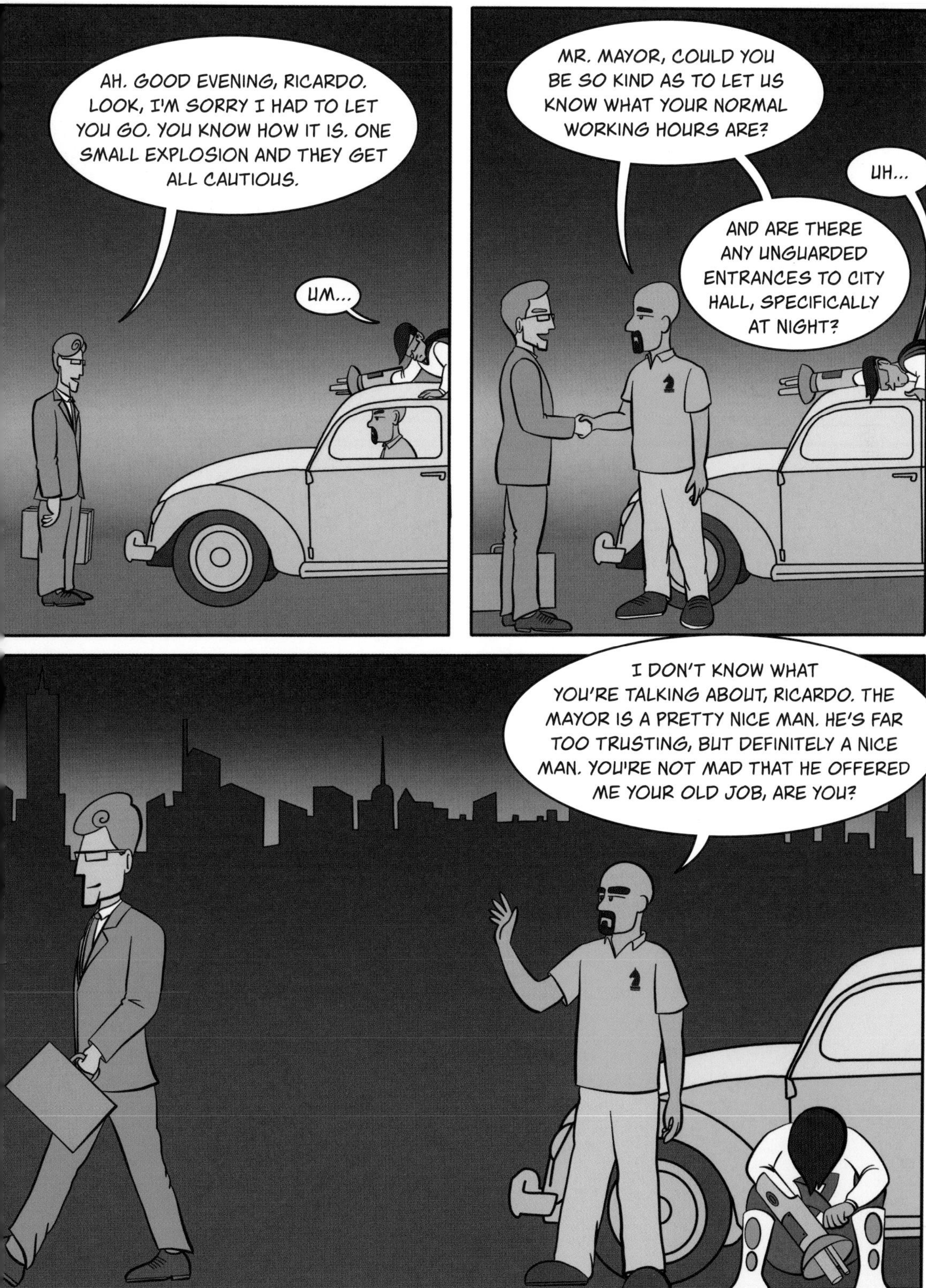
AH. GOOD EVENING, RICARDO. LOOK, I'M SORRY I HAD TO LET YOU GO. YOU KNOW HOW IT IS. ONE SMALL EXPLOSION AND THEY GET ALL CAUTIOUS.
UM...
MR. MAYOR, COULD YOU BE SO KIND AS TO LET US KNOW WHAT YOUR NORMAL WORKING HOURS ARE?
AND ARE THERE ANY UNGUARDED ENTRANCES TO CITY HALL, SPECIFICALLY AT NIGHT?
UH...
I DON'T KNOW WHAT YOU'RE TALKING ABOUT, RICARDO. THE MAYOR IS A PRETTY NICE MAN. HE'S FAR TOO TRUSTING, BUT DEFINITELY A NICE MAN. YOU'RE NOT MAD THAT HE OFFERED ME YOUR OLD JOB, ARE YOU?

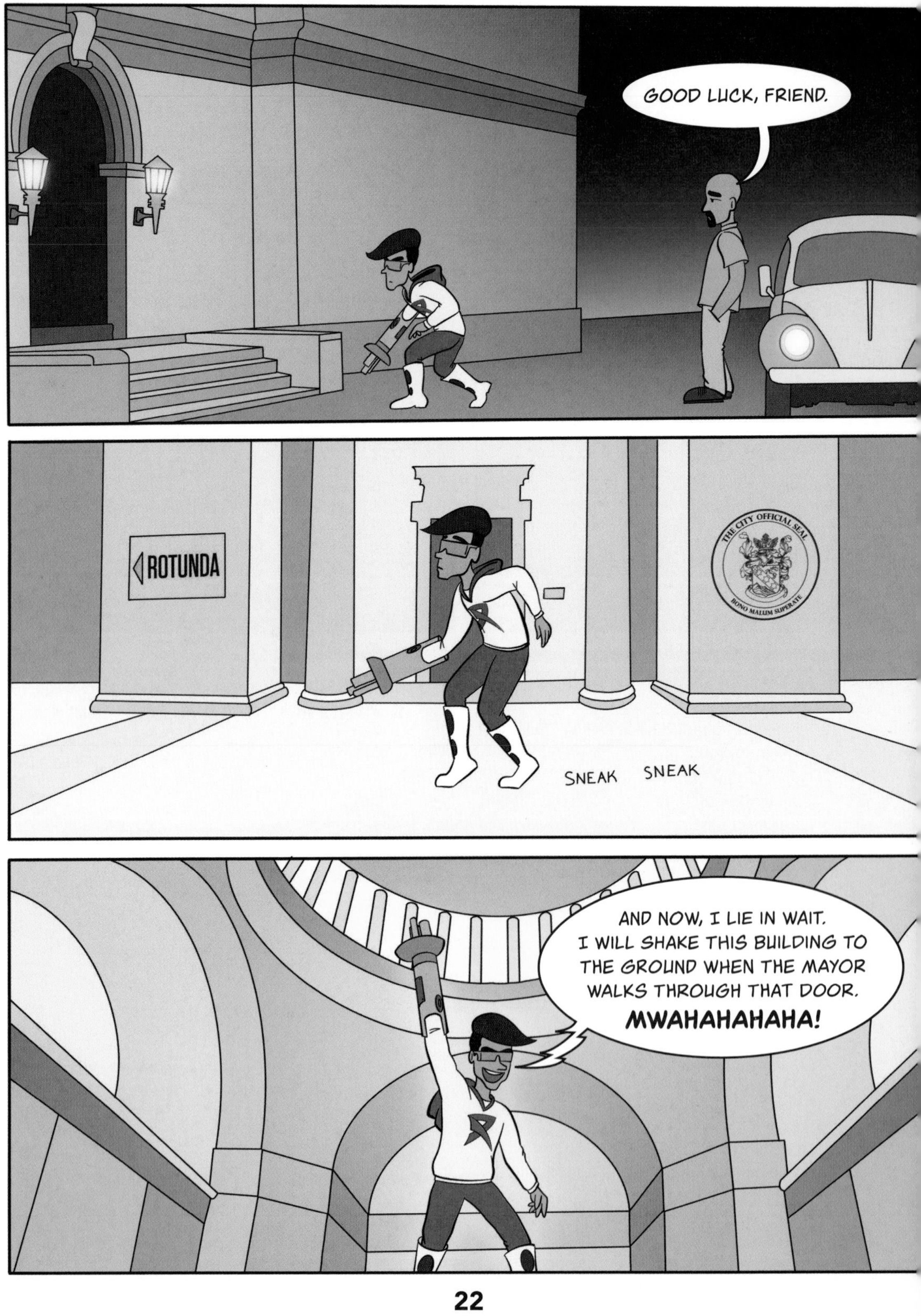
GOOD LUCK, FRIEND.
ROTUNDA
THE CITY OFFICIAL SEAL
BONO MALUM SUPERATE
SNEAK SNEAK
AND NOW, I LIE IN WAIT. I WILL SHAKE THIS BUILDING TO THE GROUND WHEN THE MAYOR WALKS THROUGH THAT DOOR. **MWAHAHAHAHA!**

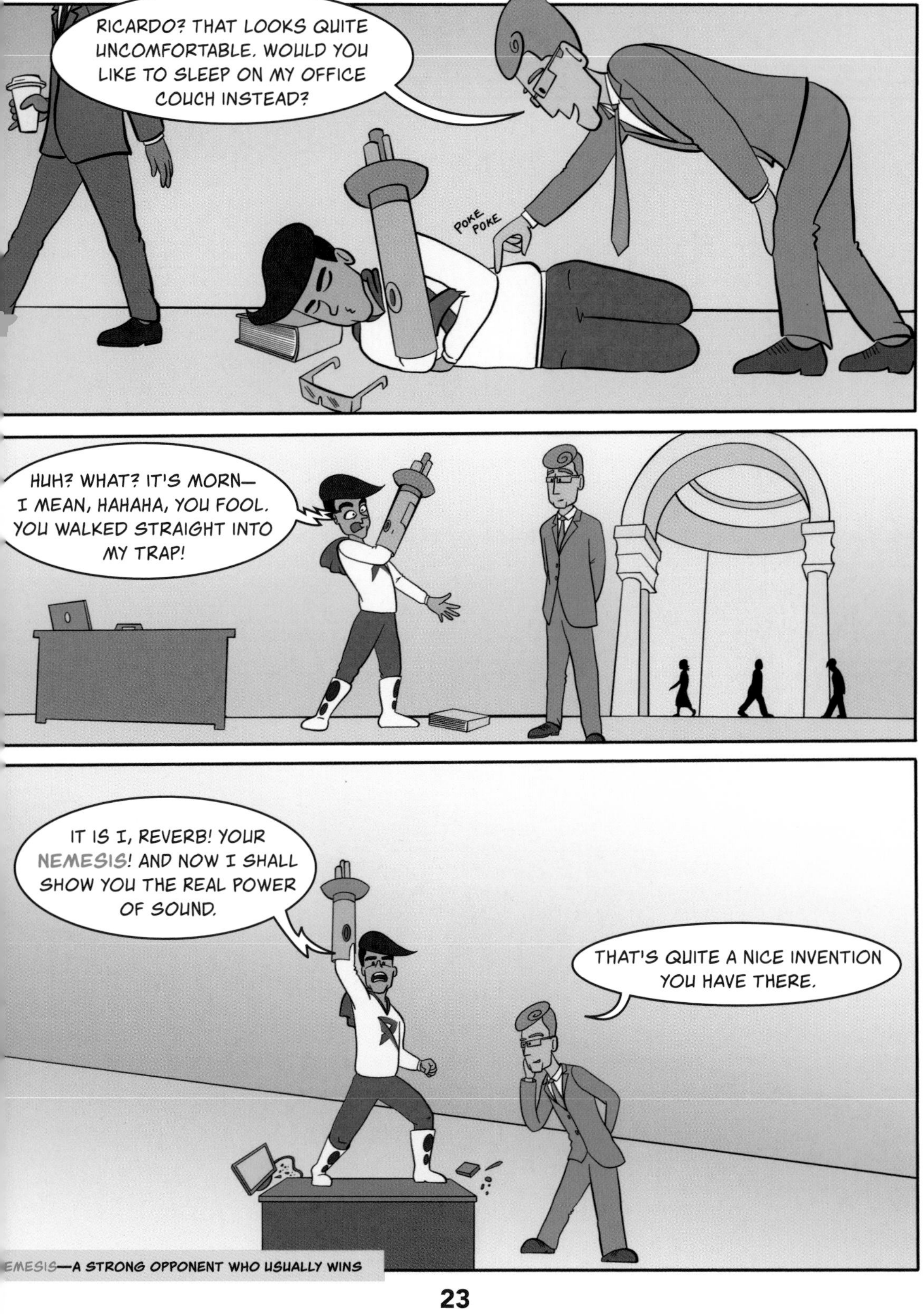
RICARDO? THAT LOOKS QUITE UNCOMFORTABLE. WOULD YOU LIKE TO SLEEP ON MY OFFICE COUCH INSTEAD?
POKE POKE
HUH? WHAT? IT'S MORN— I MEAN, HAHAHA, YOU FOOL. YOU WALKED STRAIGHT INTO MY TRAP!
IT IS I, REVERB! YOUR NEMESIS! AND NOW I SHALL SHOW YOU THE REAL POWER OF SOUND.
THAT'S QUITE A NICE INVENTION YOU HAVE THERE.

EMESIS—A STRONG OPPONENT WHO USUALLY WINS

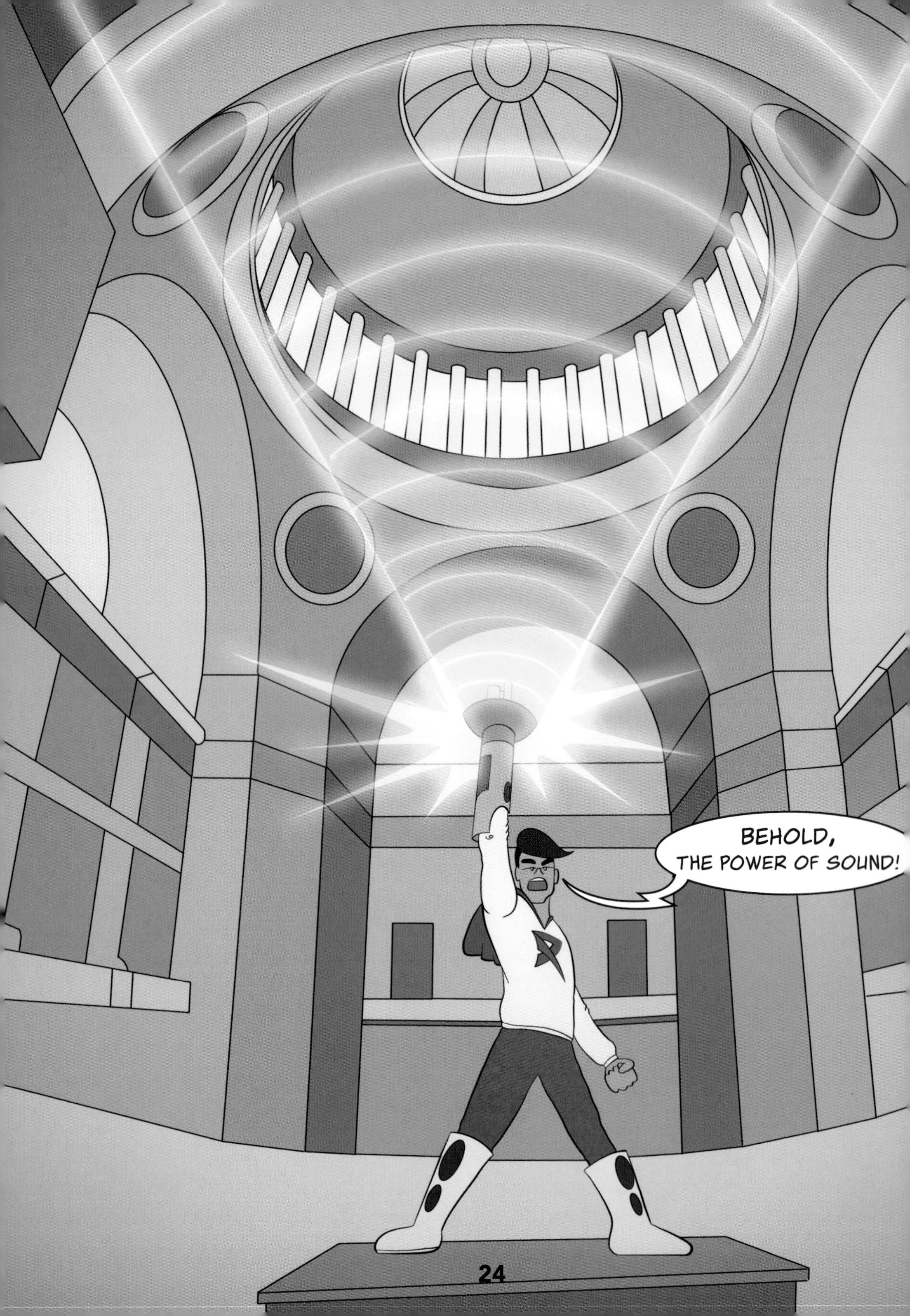
BEHOLD,
THE POWER OF SOUND!

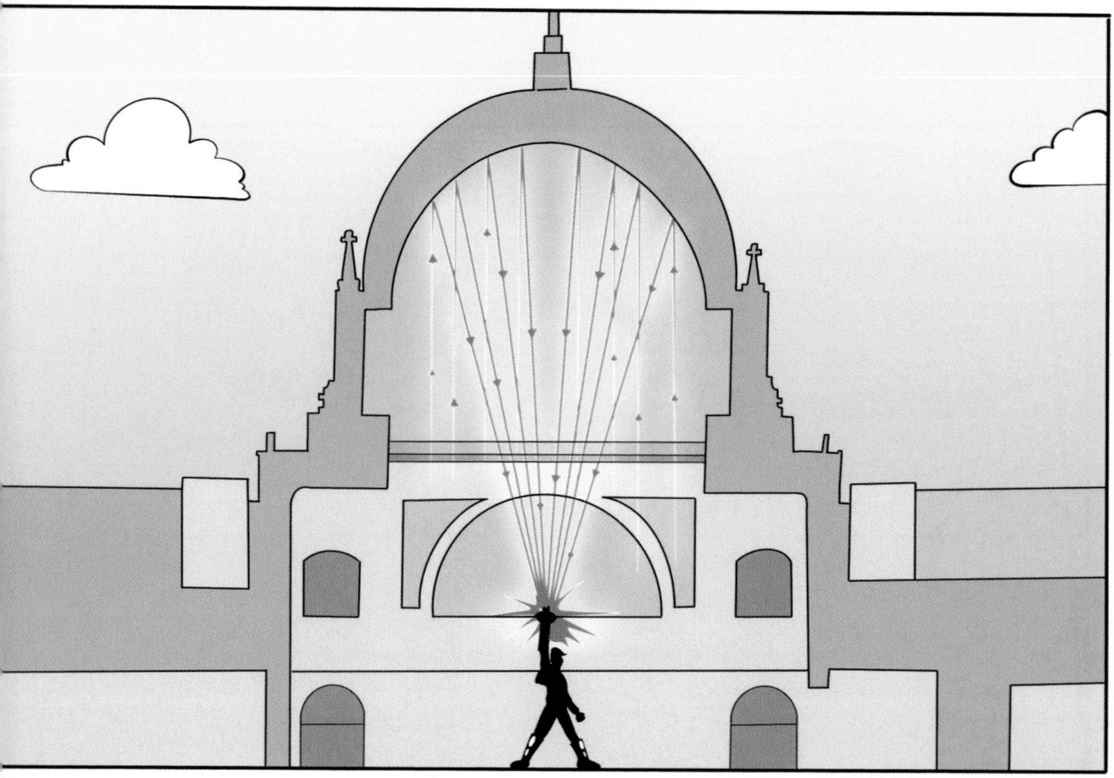

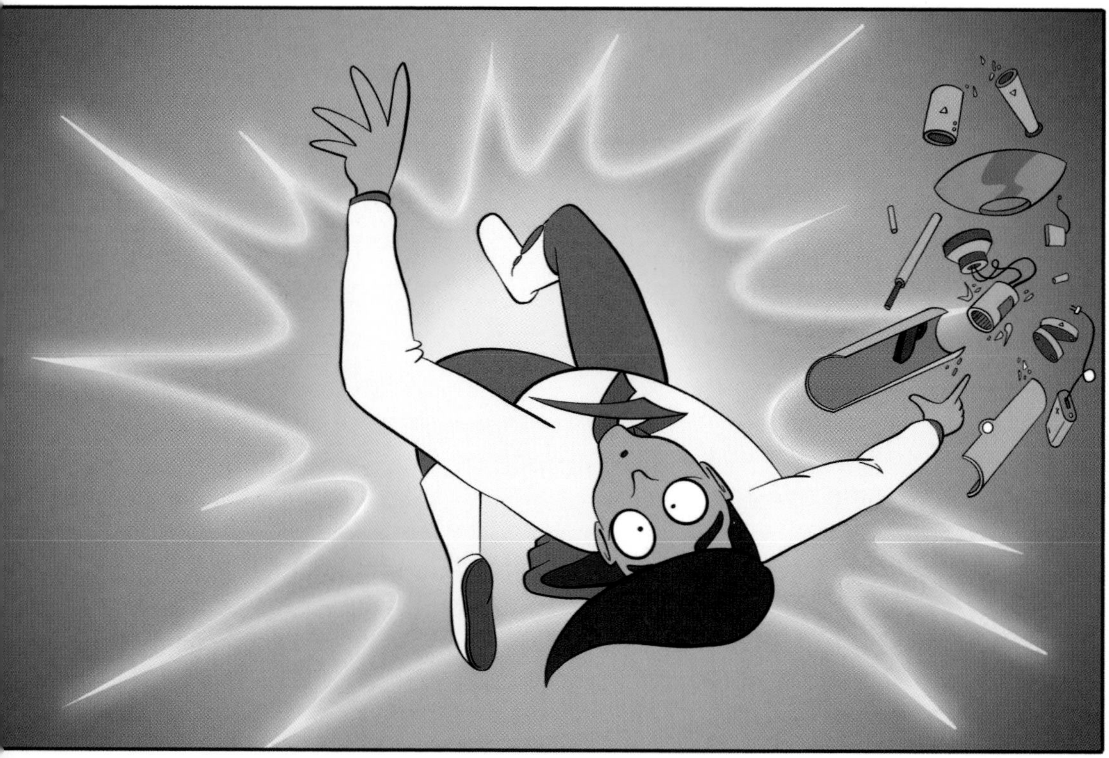

Whisper Dishes

Parabolic reflectors are conical-shaped objects used to collect or project different energy sources such as light or sound. Conical means having the shape of a cone. When parabolic reflectors are used, faint noises from great distances can be heard. Whisper dishes are a special kind of parabolic reflector that contains two different size dishes: a large main dish and a smaller focus dish at its center. This setup allows for the collection, focus, amplification, and redirection of incoming sources of sound waves to another whisper dish.

When incoming sound waves make contact with one whisper dish, these waves are reflected and redirected toward that dish's focal point. Because of the shape of the dish, the sound wave then bounces over to a separate whisper dish a good distance away. If you were to whisper into one dish, your friend standing at the other dish could hear what you've said as if you were right there! Whisper dishes have been used in a variety of applications, including parabolic microphones, aircraft detection, and even exhibits in science museums!

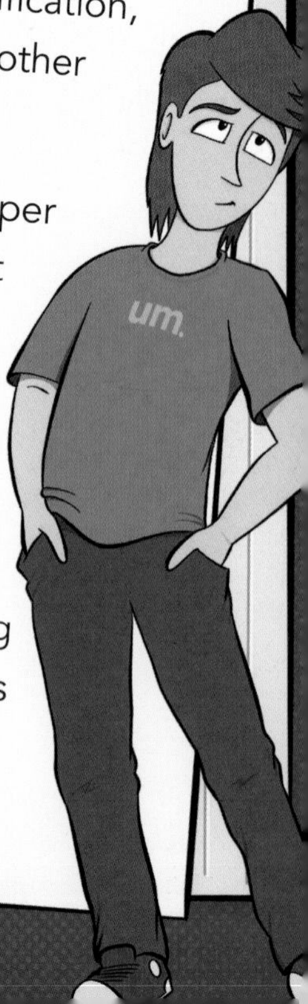
um.

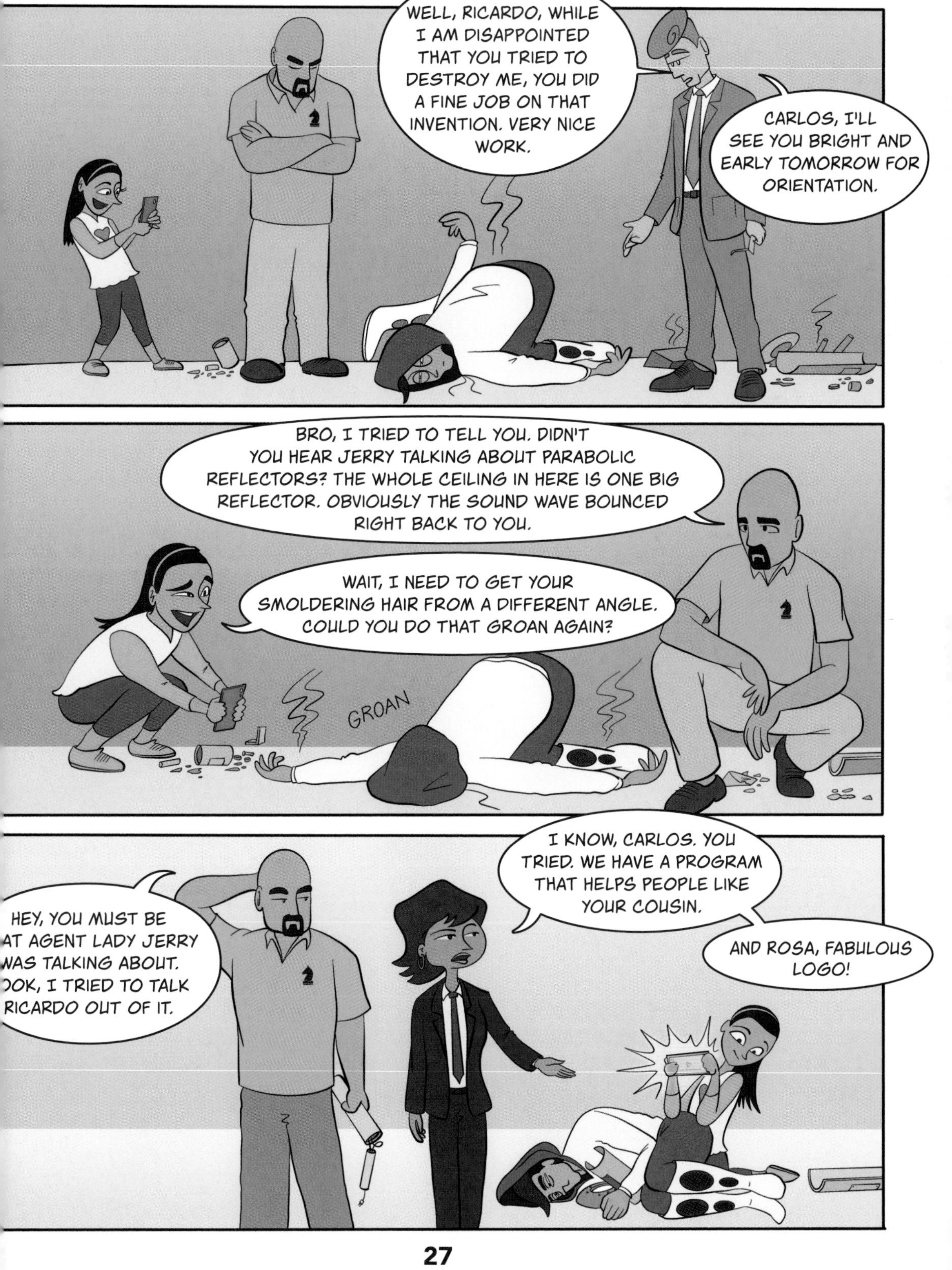
WELL, RICARDO, WHILE I AM DISAPPOINTED THAT YOU TRIED TO DESTROY ME, YOU DID A FINE JOB ON THAT INVENTION. VERY NICE WORK.
CARLOS, I'LL SEE YOU BRIGHT AND EARLY TOMORROW FOR ORIENTATION.
BRO, I TRIED TO TELL YOU. DIDN'T YOU HEAR JERRY TALKING ABOUT PARABOLIC REFLECTORS? THE WHOLE CEILING IN HERE IS ONE BIG REFLECTOR. OBVIOUSLY THE SOUND WAVE BOUNCED RIGHT BACK TO YOU.
WAIT, I NEED TO GET YOUR SMOLDERING HAIR FROM A DIFFERENT ANGLE. COULD YOU DO THAT GROAN AGAIN?
GROAN
HEY, YOU MUST BE AT AGENT LADY JERRY WAS TALKING ABOUT. OOK, I TRIED TO TALK RICARDO OUT OF IT.
I KNOW, CARLOS. YOU TRIED. WE HAVE A PROGRAM THAT HELPS PEOPLE LIKE YOUR COUSIN.
AND ROSA, FABULOUS LOGO!

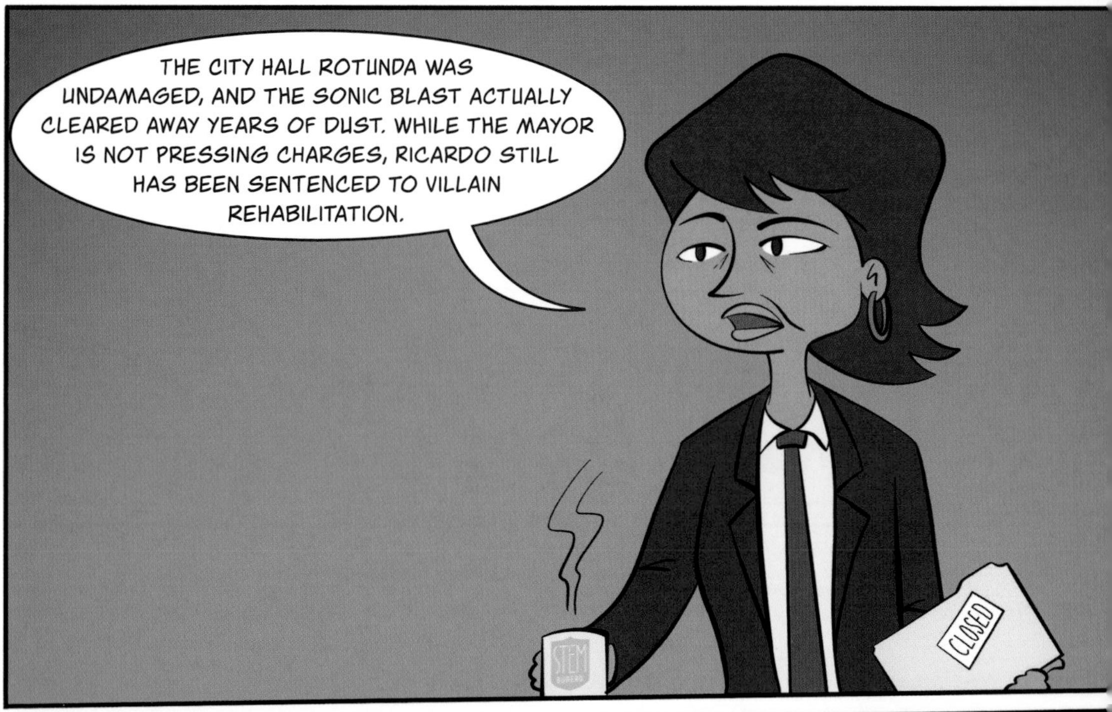
THE CITY HALL ROTUNDA WAS UNDAMAGED, AND THE SONIC BLAST ACTUALLY CLEARED AWAY YEARS OF DUST. WHILE THE MAYOR IS NOT PRESSING CHARGES, RICARDO STILL HAS BEEN SENTENCED TO VILLAIN REHABILITATION.
STEM
CLOSED

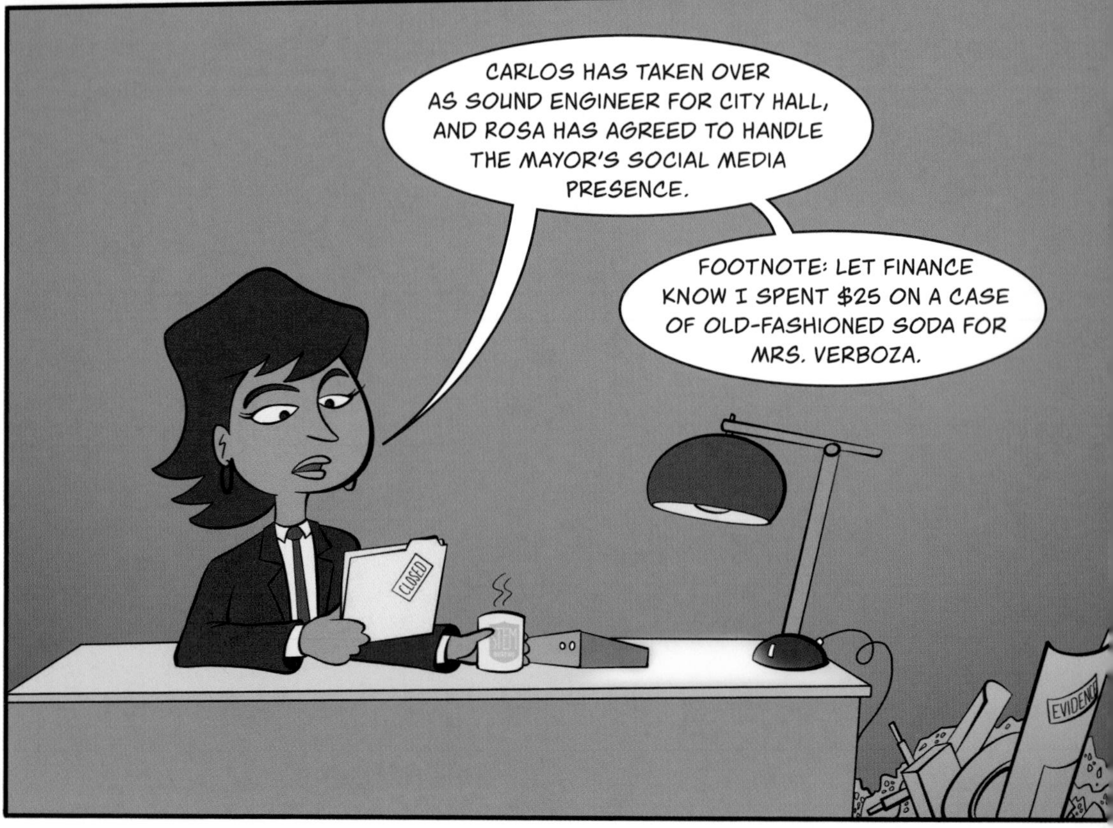
CARLOS HAS TAKEN OVER AS SOUND ENGINEER FOR CITY HALL, AND ROSA HAS AGREED TO HANDLE THE MAYOR'S SOCIAL MEDIA PRESENCE.
FOOTNOTE: LET FINANCE KNOW I SPENT $25 ON A CASE OF OLD-FASHIONED SODA FOR MRS. VERBOZA.
CLOSED
STEM
EVIDENCE

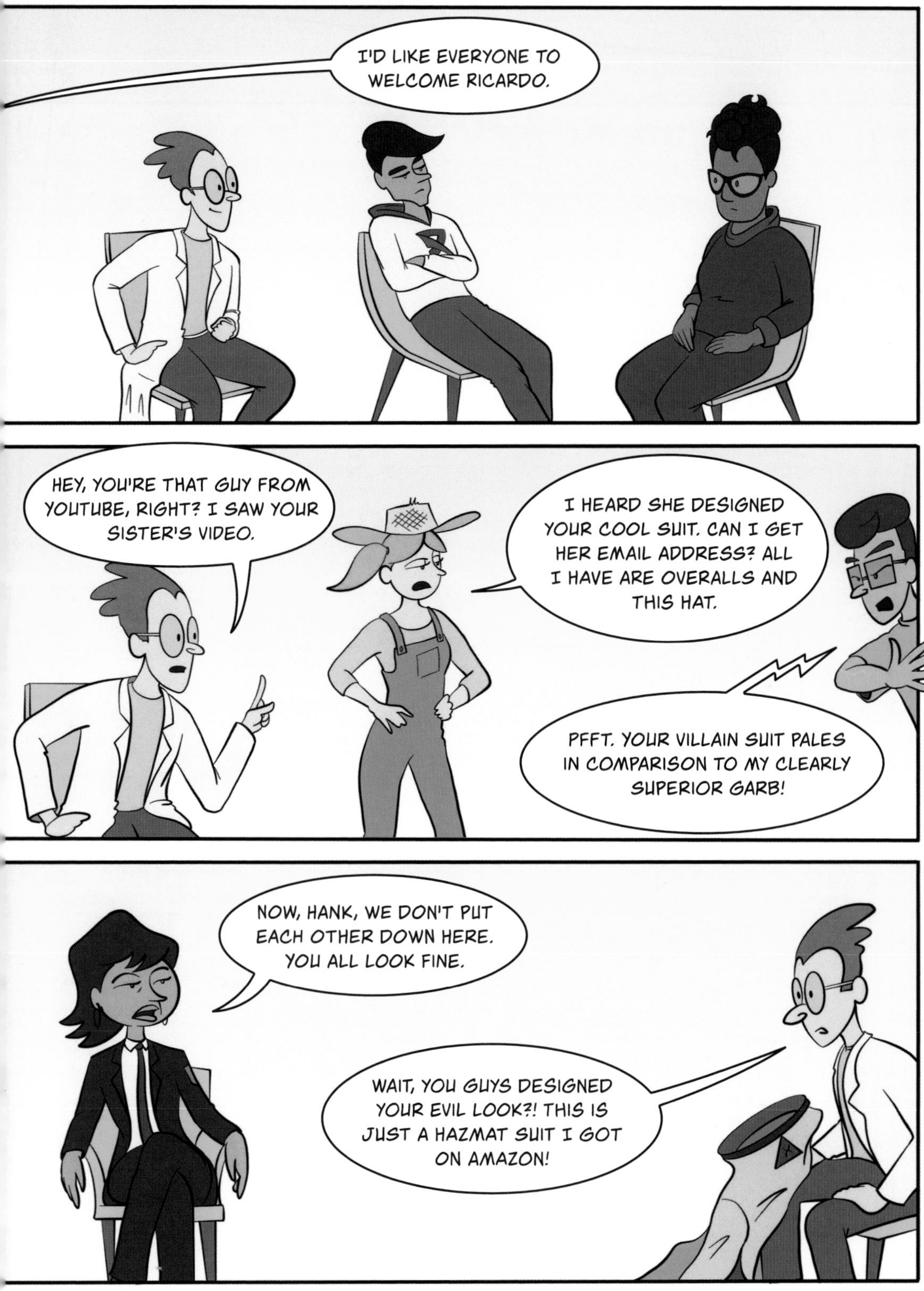
I'D LIKE EVERYONE TO WELCOME RICARDO.
HEY, YOU'RE THAT GUY FROM YOUTUBE, RIGHT? I SAW YOUR SISTER'S VIDEO.
I HEARD SHE DESIGNED YOUR COOL SUIT. CAN I GET HER EMAIL ADDRESS? ALL I HAVE ARE OVERALLS AND THIS HAT.
PFFT. YOUR VILLAIN SUIT PALES IN COMPARISON TO MY CLEARLY SUPERIOR GARB!
NOW, HANK, WE DON'T PUT EACH OTHER DOWN HERE. YOU ALL LOOK FINE.
WAIT, YOU GUYS DESIGNED YOUR EVIL LOOK?! THIS IS JUST A HAZMAT SUIT I GOT ON AMAZON!

Infrasound and Ultrasound

Although the human ear is capable of hearing a wide range of sounds, there are noises that exist outside this range that cannot be heard. Two of these types of sounds are infrasound and ultrasound.

Infrasounds are low-frequency sounds that occur below 20 Hertz. Hertz (Hz) is the unit used to measure sound. Most humans cannot hear below 20 Hz. Examples of infrasound include naturally produced noises from severe weather storms, earthquakes, and volcanoes. Some animals, like whales, elephants, and alligators, communicate using infrasound. On the other hand, ultrasounds are high-frequency sounds that occur above 20,000 Hz. Most humans cannot hear above 20,000 Hz. Ultrasounds are typically used for seeing inside the human body. In nature, certain animals, including dolphins and bats, use ultrasound to navigate.

Glossary

acoustic (uh-KOO-stik) relating to sound

amplifier (AM-pluh-fye-ur) a device to boost a weak signal without changing it

carnivorous (kahr-NIV-ur-uhs) meat eating

feedback (FEED-bak) an unwanted sound caused by an electronic sound system

mija (MEE-hah) a term of affection in Spanish that means "my daughter"

mijo (MEE-hoh) a term of affection in Spanish that means "my son"

mitigation (mit-uh-GAY-shuhn) the act of making something less dangerous or damaging

nemesis (NEM-uh-ses) a strong opponent who usually wins

parabolic reflector (par-uh-BAH-lik rih-FLEK-tur) a curved surface meant to collect and reflect waves

reverb (REE-vurb) an echo sound effect

sonic (SAH-nik) relating to sound waves

strategic (struh-TEE-jik) useful or important in achieving a plan or strategy

Index

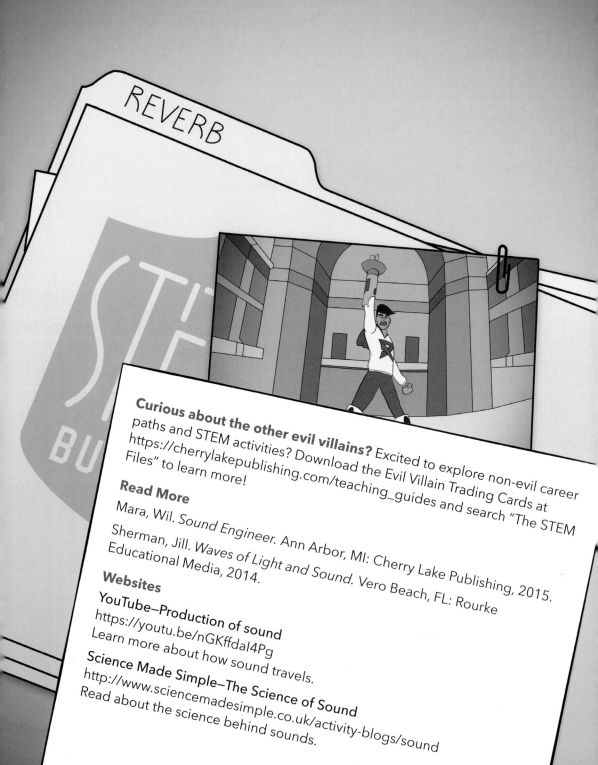

Curious about the other evil villains? Excited to explore non-evil career paths and STEM activities? Download the Evil Villain Trading Cards at https://cherrylakepublishing.com/teaching_guides and search "The STEM Files" to learn more!

Read More

Mara, Wil. *Sound Engineer.* Ann Arbor, MI: Cherry Lake Publishing, 2015.

Sherman, Jill. *Waves of Light and Sound.* Vero Beach, FL: Rourke Educational Media, 2014.

Websites

YouTube—Production of sound
https://youtu.be/nGKffdaI4Pg
Learn more about how sound travels.

Science Made Simple—The Science of Sound
http://www.sciencemadesimple.co.uk/activity-blogs/sound
Read about the science behind sounds.